Praise for *The Undertaking*

"The year in literature may not produce a better opening line—'Every year I bury a couple hundred of my townspeople'—and the rest of *The Undertaking* lives up to that earthshaking start . . . 'A memoir that is standout superb even in an era thick with first personages."
—*Esquire*

"Lynch's essays are consistently humane and observant of the tragic, humorous, and occasionally startling vagaries of human life. . . . Highly recommended reading for fans of poetry, Ireland, funeral and cultural customs, or anything else. More than a study of 'the dismal trade,' it is a long view of what it means to be human."   —*Detroit Free Press*

"[An] unusual and affecting book. Lynch writes beautifully and affectingly . . . Each of the book's chapters . . . enchants and instructs while enlightening us in the ways of living, dying, and most important, in Lynch's anything-but-dismal view, loving."   —*Elle*

"A startling and eloquent meditation on death and bereavement. . . . If you think this book isn't about you, or for you, think again."
—*Spin*

"There are sad, sad stories in this book, and there are noble moments to match. . . . His humor is as black as Jonathan Swift and as swift as S.J. Perelman's."   —*USA Today*

"One of the most life-affirming books I have read in a long time . . . brims with humanity, irreverence, and invigorating candor."
—Tom Vanderbilt, *The Nation*

"He is able to take us inside the palpable business of blood, tears, and the final verse of life in a manner that is almost shocking in the relief it delivers. . . . [A] fine, sensible, and wise book."   —*The Boston Sunday Globe*

"[Lynch] devotes most of his finely composed pages to gently humorous and unabashedly affectionate portraits of the people he loves. . . . [A] collection of powerful and cadenced essays."   —*Chicago Tribune*

"All of the tales are as morbidly fascinating as the sheet-covered form lying next to the wreck on the highway; *The Undertaking* is to die for."
—*People*

"Remarkable . . . [Lynch] writes in a disarmingly wry and tender way."
—*Utne Reader*

"He brings the lessons of death to life, and turns life and death into art."
—*Time Out New York*

"[Lynch is] a poet who brings considerable skills of voice and tone to a series of interrelated essays on his work."   —*Bloomsbury Review*

Life Studies from the Dismal Trade

THE
UNDERTAKING

Thomas Lynch

PENGUIN BOOKS

PENGUIN BOOKS

Published by the Penguin Group

Penguin Group (USA) Inc., 375 Hudson Street, New York, New York 10014, U.S.A.

Penguin Group (Canada), 90 Eglinton Avenue East, Suite 700, Toronto,
   Ontario, Canada M4P 2Y3 (a division of Pearson Penguin Canada Inc.)

Penguin Books Ltd, 80 Strand, London WC2R 0RL, England

Penguin Ireland, 25 St Stephen's Green, Dublin 2, Ireland (a division of Penguin Books Ltd)

Penguin Group (Australia), 250 Camberwell Road, Camberwell,
   Victoria 3124, Australia (a division of Pearson Australia Group Pty Ltd)

Penguin Books India Pvt Ltd, 11 Community Centre, Panchsheel Park, New Delhi – 110 017, India

Penguin Group (NZ), cnr Airborne and Rosedale Roads,
   Albany, Auckland 1310, New Zealand (a division of Pearson New Zealand Ltd)

Penguin Books (South Africa) (Pty) Ltd, 24 Sturdee Avenue,
   Rosebank, Johannesburg 2196, South Africa

Penguin Books Ltd, Registered Offices: 80 Strand, London WC2R 0RL, England

First published in the United States of America by
W.W. Norton & Company, Inc. 1997
Published in Penguin Books 1998

20 19 18

Acknowledgment is made to the following for permission to reprint: Lines from
"Old Life," by Donald Hall excerpted from *The Old Life*. Copyright © 1996 by
Donald Hall. Reprinted by permission of Houghton Mifflin Company. All rights
reserved. "Notes from the Other Side" copyright 1996 by Jane Kenyon. Reprinted
from *Otherwise New & Selected Poems* with the permission of Graywolf Press, Saint
Paul, Minnesota. William Carlos Williams: *Collected Poems: 1909–1939*, Volume 1
© copyright 1938 by New Directions Publishing Corporation. Reprinted by permission of New Directions Publishing Corporation.

THE LIBRARY OF CONGRESS HAS CATALOGUED THE HARDCOVER AS FOLLOWS:
Lynch, Thomas, 1948–
The undertaking : life studies from the dismal trade/Thomas Lynch.
   p.   cm.
ISBN 0-393-04112-3 (hc.)
ISBN 0 14 02.7623 8 (pbk.)
1. Death.   2. Grief.   3. Lynch, Thomas, 1948–.   I. Title.
BD444.L96   1997
814´.54—dc21   96–40900

Printed in the United States of America
Text composed in Bembo with display set in Evangel
Designed by Judith Stagnitto Abbate

This book is for
Dan, Pat, Tim, Mary, Julie, Eddie, Chris, and Brigid

~

In Memory of Our Parents
Rosemary O'Hara and Edward Joseph Lynch

Now there is no more catching
one's own eye in the mirror,

The poor we no longer have with us.
Our calm hearts strike only the hour,

and God, as promised, proves
to be mercy clothed in light.

—JANE KENYON
1948–1995

~

Sunt lacrimae rerum et mentem mortalia tangunt.

—VIRGIL
70–19 B.C.

~

And I swear that I don't have a gun.
No I don't have a gun.

—KURT D. COBAIN
1967–1994

~

I chose the Vermont Hardwood,
dark and shiny. At calling hours
we said that her mouth
was wrong. It was a comfort, I suppose.

—DONALD HALL

Acknowledgments

Thanks are due to John Lanchester of *The London Review of Books* and Alexandra Ringe of *Harper's* for the early publication of several of the essays that appear in this collection. To Gordon Lish, who published my first poems and essays, I owe permanent thanks. As I do to Jill Bialosky at W. W. Norton whose trust in and efforts on behalf of this manuscript have brought it into being.

I shall always be in arrears in my indebtedness to Robin Robertson at Jonathan Cape, well met in Dublin in the Spring of 1989, who has edited my poems and who first suggested a book of this type over raw fish in London a few years ago.

Likewise, I am grateful to my agent, Richard P. McDonough, for his championship of this manuscript and his loyalty and friendship.

Thanks also to the men and women at Lynch & Sons Funeral Directors with whom I work. Their dedication and professionalism have afforded me the time to complete this book. Especial thanks are due to my brother Edward, whose duties have redoubled in my absences. He is, like the man he was named for, a true caregiver, a good and decent man. I am grateful, also, to my neighbors and friends in Highland Township and Milford, Michigan, for entrusting to our family, for nearly twenty-five years now, the care of their families in difficult times. By sharing with me the details of their lives and deaths, they have made me aware of just how precious we are to one another. In the preparation of these essays, I have been keenly aware of the obligation to respect their privacy. Thus, some of the events and characters recorded here are composites, cominglings—truths renamed, reshaped, refaced, but finally told, in ways that protect the trust they've given me.

For related reasons, I am ever in the debt of writers and friends, Irish, English, Scots, and Americans, who have let me write, sometimes fast and loose, about our friendships.

I am thankful to Pat Lynch, Mary Howell, Melissa Weisberg, Audrey Kowalski, and Fr. Matthew Lawrence, each of whom read and gave valuable commentary on this manuscript in its making.

To Karen O'Connor of WGBH in Boston and the office of the Oakland County Medical Examiner, I am indebted for material mentioned in *Uncle Eddie, Inc.* Also, to Ron Willis, cemetery sexton and thinking man, I owe thanks for his willingness and ability to take the other side of any argument, without which my own would never approach clarity.

To my daughter, Heather Grace, and my sons Tom, Mike, and Sean, I am ever beholden for their patience, enduring, as they do, draft after draft of a work in progress.

No vocabulary of thanks and praise includes the words sufficient for what I owe to Mary Tata who has known this text from the very first.

Contents

Preface

‿

At first I thought it meant he took them under. It was the fifties and I was the child, one of several as it turned out, of an undertaker. This was a fact of greater matter to the kids I hung out with than to me.

"What does he *do*?" one would ask. "How does he *do* it?"

I said I thought it had to do with holes, with digging holes. And there were bodies involved. Dead bodies.

"He takes them *under*. Get it? Under *ground*."

This would usually shut them up.

Still, I wasn't as certain as I tried to sound. And I wondered why it wasn't *underputter*—you know, for the one who *puts* them underground. Surely to *take* them seemed a bit excessive. I mean if they were dead. They wouldn't need the company on the way. Like you would *take* your sister to the drug store but you would *put* your bike in the garage. I loved the play of words and the meanings of them.

At seven I was sent to learn the Latin required of an altar boy. It was my mother's idea. She said if I was stingy with God, God would be stingy with me. This had the ring, if not of truth, then of my mother's will, which was, to me, the nearest thing to truth. The Latin was magic and mysterious—the acoustics made rich by its abundant vowels. Every Tuesday at four o'clock I'd meet with Fr. Kenny from St. Columban's to learn the ancient syllables by heart. He'd given me a card with the priest's part in red and my part in black. He had come from Ireland and had been at seminary with my father's uncle: a priest who died young of tuberculosis, after whom I was named. I was vaguely aware of a conspiracy hatched between my mother and Fr. Kenny that would eventuate in my ordination. I heard a full confession of the particulars from Fr. Kenny himself, years later, after he'd retired and returned to Salthill in Galway. The world and the church had changed too much for him.

I remember him meeting my father at the back of church. I was always released from school to serve the funerals. My father, impeccable in morning dress, the pallbearers—gloved and boutonniered—the brown casket, the sniffling family and friends behind it.

They'd changed the vestments from black to white. Englished everything. Revised the rules. Fr. Kenny did not approve of change.

"Edward" he bellowed when he reached the back, "I'm told we are to *celebrate* this funeral. So wipe the solemn fellow off your face and kindly instruct Mrs. Grimaldi that the Cardinal expects her to cheer up for her husband's funeral."

The Grimaldi entourage, accustomed to Fr. Kenny's sarcasm, looked anything but in the mood.

I stood, cassocked and surpliced between the priest and my father, holding the bucket of holy water.

"Next thing you know we'll be *grieving* the baptisms . . .," Fr. Kenny was warming to his theme.

"Time now, Father," my father said.

Then the priest, looking indignant in his white chasuble, sprinkled the casket with holy water and turned toward the altar where the organist had begun some upbeat number from the new hymnal. Fr. Kenny hushed him with a hard glance, breathed deeply through his nostrils, and intoned the doleful comforts of *In Paradisum* in the sad tenor he had brought from home.

He knew that nothing would ever be the same.

By such instructions I had come to know that the undertaking that my father did had less to do with what was done to the dead and more to do with what the living did about the fact of life that people died.

In the wordsmithing of the day, new names for what he did were made.

Mortician he could not abide because it made it sound like something scientific or new-fangled, like the cars and TVs and appliances, perennially repackaged, renewed, and improved.

Funeral director sounded sensible. He had all the signs changed from Funeral Home to Funeral Directors, believing that it was the people, not the place, that folks in trouble counted on.

But in the mirror he saw an undertaker—someone who stood with the living confronted with death and pledged to do whatever could be done about it. The undertaking was nothing new. It was as old, he figured, as life itself.

My pals still wanted grim details.

"The facts . . .," as Joe Friday always said, "just the facts."

And so we huddled with my father's *Gray's Anatomy* and Bell's *Pathology*—books he'd bought in mortuary school—wincing over pictures of disfigurement, disease, and death the way we would later with pornography.

But the facts were largely disappointing. No one sat up in their caskets. No one had seen a ghost. I hadn't noticed if fingernails or hair continued to grow. Rigor mortis wasn't all that special. The dead were unremarkable in ways that were hard to imagine.

Not so the living. Not so the glossy women in the girlie mags. Not so the life that seemed more wondrous and more monstrous as we came of age.

Maybe it is so for every generation—that sex and death are the required lessons.

My parents, ever sweethearts, graduated high school in time for World War II. My mother went to college and worked in a hospital. My father went with the First Marines to the South Pacific, then to China, then home when it was over. Their world seemed full of possibilities. Their sexuality, sharpened by hunger and the brush with death, put off by threats of pregnancy, postponed by war, found its blossom in the Baby Boom. Sex and death for them were antonyms. Straight shooters and villains, virgins and whores, the right and the wrong crowd— the pictures we have of them are black and white. Known for their romance and fidelities, the children of great wars and great depression hankered for security, safety, and permanence, wise investments and a piece of the rock. They married forever, moved to the suburbs, and lived as if they never had to die.

My generation, those boomers, born with the nuclear gun to its head, raised with it cocked in Cuba and Berlin, saw love and death like cartoons on TV. We watched the sky. We watched the news. We played in bomb-shelters. And just as we were getting out of or going into puberty, the hammer dropped on Kennedy. That Friday in high school or in junior high we turned from fantasies of chests and pelvises, the bright new body parts of our youth and desires, to consider the first death in our lives that took. Was it this coincidence of sex and death, of creative and deadly forces in our lives that made our lives and deaths seem random after that? Spontaneous, casual, unpredictable, disconnected from our gravity, we grabbed all the gusto we could get. We only were going round once in this life. If we couldn't be with the one we loved, honey, we loved the one we were with. Then and now we age with the grace (in Cummings' careful metaphor) of polar bears on rollerskates. Wary of being caught unawares, we planned our parenthood, committed to trial marriages with pre-nuptials, and pre-arranged our parents' funerals—convinced we could pre-feel the feelings that we have heard attend new life, true love, and death. And for all our planning, for all our micromanagement, for all our yammering about our parents' mistakes, we abort more, divorce more, and soon will *kevork* more than any twenty generations on the globe before us. (The verb form of kevorkian, which proceeds from the infinitive "to kevork" should observe the usage guides applied, in practice, to the other high-volume verb of our generation—a verb I never, as a matter of style, deploy whenever lesser words will do, in the hopes that it, unlike certain antibiotics, will maintain its punch—to wit: "kevork off" or "go kevork yourself" or "take that you mother-kevorker" or in the rhetorical "are you out of your kevorking mind?")

But for my daughter and my sons, I fear that sex and death are nearly synonyms. They rhyme too well to be that far removed. Sex is, for them, an odd game of roulette, a deadly lotto on which we figure odds for safe, safer, and safest sex (which is the name we give to none). And death for them? A kind of yawner—a little excitement for those who can't be shocked. A lapse of caution in which full and fatal contact is finally made. Is safe that much better than sorry? Really? Wow! Kurt Cobain grins at them on the wall. "I wonder if he *felt* it," someone says.

They inhabit a world so rich in technology that everything works better, even the people, but no one seems to know exactly why. Parented by proxy and prescription and by cable TV, they have achieved the loneliness their elders pursued. They enter their twenties less interested in finding themselves than in finding the way out. Faithless, hopeless, untutored in love, they make babies for the sake of company and kill themselves with unspeakable violence in staggering numbers—suffering from a deficiency in meaning acquired from pop culture, pop psychology, feel-good religion, that tells them don't worry, be happy, take care of yourself and your self-esteem. They stand to inherit, along with the spiritual void their parents have left them, the bill from the card it was all charged to.

Watching my parents, I watched the meaning change, of what it was that undertakers do: From something done with the dead, to something done for the living, to something done by the living—everyone of us.

After high school, I registered for the draft, enrolled in a college, and waited for life to happen to me. I worked at the funeral home. I worked at the state asylum. I worked at a home for alcoholic priests. I learned to drink. I fell in love. Friends of mine had died in Vietnam. The possibilities seemed frightening.

I went to Ireland. I lived in the house my great-grandfather left a century before to come to Michigan. No phone or furnace, no plumbing or TV, no tractor or car or convenience store—the life led there seemed elemental, nearer the edges, clarified. Cows calved, neighbors died, the tidal ocean rose and fell, folks talked.

That winter and spring on the west coast of Clare my life and times began to make some sense. And though this weary century of change is having its way with even Ireland now, I return to that place as one does to a well, a source, for the sense that it gives me of something true.

Thus, undertakings are the things we do to vest the lives we lead against the cold, the meaningless, the void, the noisy blather, and the blinding dark. It is the voice we give to wonderment, to pain, to love and desire, anger and outrage; the words that we shape into song and prayer.

When I first wrote and published poems, my father asked me when I'd write a book about funerals. I said I thought I had already. He nodded, smiled. Every so often he'd ask me again. "You know what I mean," he said. I did, of course. I'd write the book sometime.

And much was made, in my books' reviews, about the odd day job—as if to say, not bad for an embalmer. "Mortician/ Poet" or "Poet/Undertaker" became the standard references. The bold print labored to catch the reader's eye: "A Corpus of

Corpses" claimed the *Observer*. "Come Into My Parlour" said the *TLS*. The *Washington Post* read "Poetry Comes Down to Earth." I did not object too much to this. Nice to be noticed, I told myself, even if mainly as a dancing bear. Truth told I thought the poets I knew who taught in universities or worked in the "related" fields were undertaking too—looking for meaning and voices in life and love and death. Asked why he wrote so many elegiac poems, Seamus Heaney asked if there were any poems at all, besides the elegiac ones. "Sex and death," Yeats wrote to Pound or Pound to Yeats, I can't remember now, "are the only subjects poets should write about." Sex was lovely, the dead were everywhere. Was it any different, I asked myself, for poets-slash-English professors or poets-slash-editors or poets-slash-homemakers or poets-slash-dads?

Which undertaking is it then that does not seek to make some sense of life and living, dying and the dead?

Still, my father's question was a real one. He knew how it had informed his life, shaped it, made him the husband and father and man that he was. He knew how the grief of others, the indifference of others, the despair of others, their faith and hope, the way they bought caskets and held one another, the way they sent flowers and said goodbye, how they wept and laughed and drank and ran from it, had told him something about himself, his nature, his species, and his God. I think he knew, when I moved to Milford, twenty-two years ago today, that it would shape and change and inform my life as well.

To undertake is to bind oneself to the performance of a task, to pledge or promise to get it done. And when he died, it seemed I'd done just that. I had told him I would write the book someday. The book I had in mind would be for poets, who had their questions about the things we do. Or maybe for people who read what poets wrote, and wondered what they meant, or wanted more. I think what my father had in mind was a book for dismal traders, funeral types—for men and women who dress in black, and work the weekends and the holidays, who line the cars up and lay the bodies out, who rise and go out in the dark when someone dies and someone calls for help.

Here then is that binding loosed, the not so solemn promise kept, the pledge paid up, the undertaking done.

TL
Milford, Michigan
13 June 1996

THE
UNDERTAKING

Life Studies from the Dismal Trade

The Undertaking

~

Every year I bury a couple hundred of my townspeople. Another two or three dozen I take to the crematory to be burned. I sell caskets, burial vaults, and urns for the ashes. I have a sideline in headstones and monuments. I do flowers on commission.

Apart from the tangibles, I sell the use of my building: eleven thousand square feet, furnished and fixtured with an abundance of pastel and chair rail and crown moldings. The whole lash-up is mortgaged and remortgaged well into the next century. My rolling stock includes a hearse, two Fleetwoods, and a minivan with darkened windows our pricelist calls a service vehicle and everyone in town calls the Dead Wagon.

I used to use the *unit pricing method*—the old package deal. It meant that you had only one number to look at. It was a large number. Now everything is itemized. It's the law. So now there is a long list of items and numbers and italicized disclaimers, something like a menu or the Sears Roebuck Wish Book, and sometimes the federally-mandated options begin to look like cruise control or rear-window defrost. I wear black most of the time, to keep folks in mind of the fact we're not talking Buicks here. At the bottom of the list there is still a large number.

In a good year the gross is close to a million, five percent of which we hope to call profit. I am the only undertaker in this town. I have a corner on the market.

The market, such as it is, is figured on what is called *the crude death rate*—the number of deaths every year out of every thousand persons.

Here is how it works.

Imagine a large room into which you coax one thousand people. You slam the doors in January, leaving them plenty of food and drink, color TVs, magazines, and condoms. Your sample should have an age distribution heavy on baby boomers and their children—1.2 children per boomer. Every seventh adult is an old-timer, who, if he or she wasn't in this big room, would probably be in Florida or Arizona or a nursing home. You get the idea. The group will include fifteen lawyers, one faith healer, three dozen real-estate agents, a video technician, several licensed counselors, and a Tupperware distributor. The rest will be between jobs, middle managers, ne'er-do-wells, or retired.

Now for the magic part—come late December when you throw open the doors, only 991.6, give or take, will shuffle out upright. Two hundred and sixty will now be selling Tupperware. The other 8.4 have become the crude death rate.

Here's another stat.

Of the 8.4 corpses, two-thirds will have been old-timers, five percent will be children, and the rest (slightly less than 2.5 corpses) will be boomers—realtors and attorneys likely—one of whom was, no doubt, elected to public office during the year. What's more, three will have died of cerebral-vascular or coronary difficulties, two of cancer, one each of vehicular mayhem, diabetes, and domestic violence. The spare change will be by act of God or suicide—most likely the faith healer.

The figure most often and most conspicuously missing from the insurance charts and demographics is the one I call The Big One, which refers to the number of people out of every hundred born who will die. Over the long haul, The Big One hovers right around . . . well, dead nuts on one hundred percent. If this were on the charts, they'd call it *death expectancy* and no one would buy futures of any kind. But it is a useful number and has its lessons. Maybe you will want to figure out what to do with your life. Maybe it will make you feel a certain kinship with the rest of us. Maybe it will make you hysterical. Whatever the implications of a one hundred percent death expectancy, you can calculate how big a town this is and why it produces for me a steady if unpredictable labor.

They die around the clock here, without apparent preference for a day of the week, month of the year; there is no clear favorite in the way of season. Nor does the alignment of the stars, fullness of moon, or liturgical calendar have very much to do with it. The whereabouts are neither here nor there. They go off upright or horizontally in Chevrolets and nursing homes, in bathtubs, on the interstates, in ERs, ORs, BMWs. And while it may be that we assign more equipment or more importance to deaths that create themselves in places marked by initials—ICU being somehow better than Greenbriar Convalescent Home—it is also true that the dead don't care. In this way, the dead I bury and burn are like the dead before them, for whom time and space have become mortally unimportant. This loss of interest is, in fact, one of the first sure signs that something serious is about to happen. The next thing is they quit breathing. At this point, to be sure, a *gunshot wound to the chest* or *shock and trauma* will get more ink than a CVA or ASHD, but no cause of death is any less permanent than the other. Any one will do. The dead don't care.

Nor does *who* much matter, either. To say, "I'm OK, you're OK, and by the way, he's dead!" is, for the living, a kind of comfort.

It is why we drag rivers and comb plane wrecks and bomb sites.

It is why MIA is more painful than DOA.

It is why we have open caskets and all read the obits.

Knowing is better than not knowing, and knowing it is you is terrifically better than knowing it is me. Because once I'm the dead guy, whether you're OK or he's OK won't much interest me. You can all go bag your asses, because the dead don't care.

Of course, the living, bound by their adverbs and their actuarials, still do. Now, there is the difference and why I'm in business. The living are careful and oftentimes caring. The dead are careless, or maybe it's care-less. Either way, they don't care. These are unremarkable and verifiable truths.

My former mother-in-law, herself an unremarkable and verifiable truth, was always fond of holding forth with Cagneyesque bravado—to wit: "When I'm dead, just throw me in a box and throw me in a hole." But whenever I would remind her that we did substantially that with everyone, the woman would grow sullen and a little cranky.

Later, over meatloaf and green beans, she would invariably give out with: "When I'm dead just cremate me and scatter the ashes."

My former mother-in-law was trying to make carelessness sound like fearlessness. The kids would stop eating and look at each other. The kids' mother would plead, "Oh Mom, don't talk like that." I'd take out my lighter and begin to play with it.

In the same way, the priest that married me to this woman's daughter—a man who loved golf and gold ciboria and vestments made of Irish linen; a man who drove a great black sedan with a wine-red interior and who always had his eye on the cardinal's job—this same fellow, leaving the cemetery one day, felt called upon to instruct me thus: "No bronze coffin for me. No sir! No orchids or roses or limousines. The plain pine box is the one I want, a quiet Low Mass and the pauper's grave. No pomp and circumstance."

He wanted, he explained, to be an example of simplicity, of prudence, of piety and austerity—all priestly and, apparently,

Christian virtues. When I told him that he needn't wait, that he could begin his ministry of good example even today, that he could quit the country club and do his hacking at the public links and trade his brougham for a used Chevette; that free of his Florsheims and cashmeres and prime ribs, free of his bingo nights and building funds, he could become, for Christ's sake, the very incarnation of Francis himself, or Anthony of Padua; when I said, in fact, that I would be willing to assist him in this, that I would gladly distribute his savings and credit cards among the worthy poor of the parish, and that I would, when the sad duty called, bury him for free in the manner he would have, by then, become accustomed to; when I told your man these things, he said nothing at all, but turned his wild eye on me in the way that the cleric must have looked on Sweeney years ago, before he cursed him, irreversibly, into a bird.

What I was trying to tell the fellow was, of course, that being a dead saint is no more worthwhile than being a dead philodendron or a dead angelfish. Living is the rub, and always has been. Living saints still feel the flames and stigmata of this vale of tears, the ache of chastity and the pangs of conscience. Once dead, they let their relics do the legwork, because, as I was trying to tell this priest, the dead don't care.

Only the living care.

And I am sorry to be repeating myself, but this is the central fact of my business—that there is nothing, once you are dead, that can be done *to you* or *for you* or *with you* or *about you* that will do you any good or any harm; that any damage or decency we do accrues to the living, to whom your death happens, if it really happens to anyone. The living have to live with it. You don't. Theirs is the grief or gladness your death brings. Theirs is the loss or gain of it. Theirs is the pain and the pleasure of memory. Theirs is the invoice for services rendered and theirs is the check in the mail for its payment.

And there is the truth, abundantly self-evident, that seems, now that I think of it, the one most elusive to the old in-laws, the parish priest, and to perfect strangers who are forever accosting me in barber-shops and cocktail parties and parent-teacher conferences, hell-bent or duty-bound to let me in on what it is they want done with them when they are dead.

Give it a rest is the thing I say.

Once you are dead, put your feet up, call it a day, and let the husband or the missus or the kids or a sibling decide whether you are to be buried or burned or blown out of a cannon or left to dry out in a ditch somewhere. It's not your day to watch it, because the dead don't care.

Another reason people are always rehearsing their obsequies with me has to do with the fear of death that anyone in their right mind has. It is healthy. It keeps us from playing in traffic. I say it's a thing we should pass on to the kids.

There is a belief—widespread among the women I've dated, local Rotarians, and friends of my chidren—that I, being the undertaker here, have some irregular fascination with, special interest in, inside information about, even attachment to, *the dead*. They assume, these people, some perhaps for defensible reasons, that I want their bodies.

It is an interesting concept.

But here is the truth.

Being dead is one—the worst, the last—but only one in a series of calamities that afflicts our own and several other species. The list may include, but is not limited to, gingivitis, bowel obstruction, contested divorce, tax audit, spiritual vexation, cash flow problems, political upheaval, and on and on and on some more. There is no shortage of misery. And I am no more attracted to the dead than the dentist is to your bad gums, the doctor to your rotten innards, or the accountant to your sloppy expense records. I have no more stomach for misery that the banker or the lawyer, the pastor or the politico—because misery is careless and is everywhere. Misery is the bad

check, the ex-spouse, the mob in the street, and the IRS—
who, like the dead, feel nothing and, like the dead, *don't care*.

Which is not to say that the dead do not matter.

They do. They do. Of course they do.

Last Monday morning Milo Hornsby died. Mrs. Hornsby
called at 2 A.M. to say that Milo had *expired* and would I take
care of it, as if his condition were like any other that could be
renewed or somehow improved upon. At 2 A.M., yanked from
my REM sleep, I am thinking, put a quarter into Milo and call
me in the morning. But Milo is dead. In a moment, in a twin-
kling, Milo has slipped irretrievably out of our reach, beyond
Mrs. Hornsby and the children, beyond the women at the
laundromat he owned, beyond his comrades at the Legion
Hall, the Grand Master of the Masonic Lodge, his pastor at
First Baptist, beyond the mailman, zoning board, town council, and Chamber of Commerce; beyond us all, and any
treachery or any kindness we had in mind for him.

Milo is dead.

X's on his eyes, lights out, curtains.

Helpless, harmless.

Milo's dead.

Which is why I do not haul to my senses, coffee and quick
shave, Homburg and great coat, warm up the Dead Wagon,
and make for the freeway in the early o'clock for Milo's sake.
Milo doesn't have any sake anymore. I go for her—for she
who has become, in the same moment and the same twin-
kling, like water to ice, the Widow Hornsby. I go for her—
because she still can cry and care and pray and pay my bill.

The hospital that Milo died in is state-of-the-art. There are
signs on every door declaring a part or a process or bodily
function. I like to think that, taken together, the words would

add up to The Human Condition, but they never do. What's left of Milo, the remains, are in the basement, between SHIP-PING & RECEIVING and LAUNDRY ROOM. Milo would like that if he were still liking things. Milo's room is called PATHOLOGY.

The medical-technical parlance of death emphasizes disorder.

We are forever dying of failures, of anomalies, of insufficiencies, of dysfunctions, arrests, accidents. These are either chronic or acute. The language of death certificates—Milo's says "Cardiopulmonary Failure"—is like the language of weakness. Likewise, Mrs. Hornsby, in her grief, will be said to be breaking down or falling apart or going to pieces, as if there were something structurally awry with her. It is as if death and grief were not part of The Order of Things, as if Milo's failure and his widow's weeping were, or ought to be, sources of embarrassment. "Doing well" for Mrs. Hornsby would mean that she is bearing up, weathering the storm, or being strong for the children. We have willing pharmacists to help her with this. Of course, for Milo, doing well would mean he was back upstairs, holding his own, keeping the meters and monitors bleeping.

But Milo is downstairs, between SHIPPING & RECEIV-ING and LAUNDRY ROOM, in a stainless-steel drawer, wrapped in white plastic top to toe, and—because of his small head, wide shoulders, ponderous belly, and skinny legs, and the trailing white binding cord from his ankles and toe tag—he looks, for all the world, like a larger than life-size sperm.

I sign for him and get him out of there. At some level, I am still thinking Milo gives a shit, which by now, of course, we all know he doesn't—because the dead don't care.

Back at the funeral home, upstairs in the embalming room, behind a door marked PRIVATE, Milo Hornsby is floating on a porcelain table under florescent lights. Unwrapped, outstretched, Milo is beginning to look a little more like himself—eyes wide open, mouth agape, returning to our gravity. I shave him, close his eyes, his mouth. We call this *setting the fea-*

tures. These are the features—eyes and mouth—that will never look the way they would have looked in life when they were always opening, closing, focusing, signaling, telling us something. In death, what they tell us is that they will not be doing anything anymore. The last detail to be managed is Milo's hands—one folded over the other, over the umbilicus, in an attitude of ease, of repose, of retirement.

They will not be doing anything anymore, either.

I wash his hands before positioning them.

When my wife moved out some years ago, the children stayed here, as did the dirty laundry. It was big news in a small town. There was the gossip and the goodwill that places like this are famous for. And while there was plenty of talk, no one knew exactly what to say to me. They felt helpless, I suppose. So they brought casseroles and beef stews, took the kids out to the movies or canoeing, brought their younger sisters around to visit me. What Milo did was send his laundry van around twice a week for two months, until I found a housekeeper. Milo would pick up five loads in the morning and return them by lunchtime, fresh and folded. I never asked him to do this. I hardly knew him. I had never been in his home or his laundromat. His wife had never known my wife. His children were too old to play with my children.

After my housekeeper was installed, I went to thank Milo and pay the bill. The invoices detailed the number of loads, the washers and the dryers, detergent, bleaches, fabric softeners. I think the total came to sixty dollars. When I asked Milo what the charges were for pick-up and delivery, for stacking and folding and sorting by size, for saving my life and the lives of my children, for keeping us in clean clothes and towels and bed linen, "Never mind that" is what Milo said. "One hand washes the other."

I place Milo's right hand over his left hand, then try the other way. Then back again. Then I decide that it doesn't matter. One hand washes the other either way.

The embalming takes me about two hours.

It is daylight by the time I am done.

Every Monday morning, Ernest Fuller comes to my office. He was damaged in some profound way in Korea. The details of his damage are unknown to the locals. Ernest Fuller has no limp or anything missing so everyone thinks it was something he saw in Korea that left him a little simple, occasionally perplexed, the type to draw rein abruptly in his day-long walks, to consider the meaning of litter, pausing over bottle caps and gum wrappers. Ernest Fuller has a nervous smile and a dead-fish handshake. He wears a baseball cap and thick eyeglasses. Every Sunday night Ernest goes to the supermarket and buys up the tabloids at the checkout stands with headlines that usually involve Siamese twins or movie stars or UFOs. Ernest is a speed reader and a math whiz but because of his damage, he has never held a job and never applied for one. Every Monday morning, Ernest brings me clippings of stories under headlines like: 601 LB MAN FALLS THRU COFFIN—A GRAVE SITUA-TION or EMBALMER FOR THE STARS SAYS ELVIS IS FOREVER. The Monday morning Milo Hornsby died, Ernest's clipping had to do with an urn full of ashes, somewhere in East Anglia, that made grunting and groaning noises, that whistled sometimes, and that was expected to begin talking. Certain scientists in England could make no sense of it. They had run several tests. The ashes' widow, however, left with nine children and no estate, is convinced that her dearly beloved and greatly reduced husband is trying to give her winning numbers for the lottery. "Jacky would never leave us without good prospects," she says. "He loved his family more than anything." There is a picture of the two of them, the widow and the urn, the living and the dead, flesh and bronze, the Victrola and the Victrola's dog. She has her ear cocked, waiting.

We are always waiting. Waiting for some good word or the winning numbers. Waiting for a sign or wonder, some signal from our dear dead that the dead still care. We are gladdened when they do outstanding things, when they arise from their graves or fall through their caskets or speak to us in our waking dreams. It pleases us no end, as if the dead still cared, had agendas, were yet alive.

But the sad and well-known fact of the matter is that most of us will stay in our caskets and be dead a long time, and that our urns and graves will never make a sound. Our reason and requiems, our headstones or High Masses, will neither get us in nor keep us out of heaven. The meaning of our lives, and the memories of them, belong to the living, just as our funerals do. Whatever being the dead have now, they have by the living's faith alone.

We heat graves here for winter burials, as a kind of foreplay before digging in, to loosen the frost's hold on the ground before the sexton and his backhoe do the opening. We buried Milo in the ground on Wednesday. The mercy is that what we buried there, in an oak casket, just under the frost line, had ceased to be Milo. Milo had become the idea of himself, a permanent fixture of the third person and past tense, his widow's loss of appetite and trouble sleeping, the absence in places where we look for him, our habits of him breaking, our phantom limb, our one hand washing the other.

Gladstone

~

The undertakers are over on the other island. They are there for what is called their Midwinter Conference: the name they give to the week in February every year when funeral directors from Michigan find some warm place in the Lesser Antilles to discuss the pressing issues of their trade. The names for the workshops and seminars are borderline: "The Future of Funeral Service," "What Folks Want in a Casket," "Coping with the Cremation Crowd"—things like that. The resorts must have room service, hot tubs, good beaches, and shopping on site or nearby. No doubt it is the same for orthodontists and trial lawyers.

And I'm here on the neighboring island—a smaller place with a harbor too shallow for cruise ships and no airport. I'm a ferryboat ride from the undertakers from my home state. But I've timed my relief from the Michigan winter with theirs in case I want to register for a meeting and write off my travel. It is legal and sensible and would reduce the ultimate cost of funerals in my town where I am the funeral director and have been for nearly twenty-five years now.

But I just can't work up any enthusiasm for spending any portion of the fortnight discussing business. It's not that they aren't a great bunch, chatty and amiable as stockbrokers or insurance types; and, out of their hometowns, incognito, hell-bent on a good time, they can be downright fun, if a little bingy.

It's just that it seems I've been on a Midwinter Conference of my own for a long time. Enough is enough. I need to walk on the beach now and contemplate my next move.

My father was a funeral director and three of my five brothers are funeral directors; two of my three sisters work pre-need and bookkeeping in one of the four funeral homes around the metro area that bear our name, our father's name. It is an odd arithmetic—a kind of family farm, working the back forty of the emotional register, our livelihood depending on the deaths of others in the way that medicos depend on sickness, lawyers on crime, the clergy on the fear of God.

I can remember my mother and father going off on these Midwinter Conferences and coming back all sunburned and full of ideas and gossip about what my father insisted we call our "colleagues" rather than the "competition." He said it made us sound like doctors and lawyers, you know, professionals—people you could call in the middle of the night if there was trouble, people whose being had begun to meld with their doing, who were what they did.

Our thing—who we are, what we do—has always been about death and dying and grief and bereavement: the vulnerable underbelly of the hardier nouns: life, liberty, the pursuit of . . . well, you know. We traffic in leavetakings, goodbyes, final respects. "The last ones to let you down," my father would joke with the friends he most trusted. "Dignified Service" is what he put on the giveaway matchbooks and plastic combs and rain bonnets. And he loved to quote Gladstone, the great Victorian Liberal who sounded like a New Age Republican when he wrote that he could measure with mathematical precision a people's respect for the laws of the land by the way they cared for their dead. Of course, Gladstone inhabited a century and an England in which funerals were public and sex was private and, though the British were robbing the graves of infidels all over the world for the British Museum, they did so, by all accounts, in a mannerly fashion. I think my father first

heard about Gladstone at one of these Midwinter Conferences
and lately I've been thinking how right they were—
Gladstone, my father.

My father died three years ago tomorrow on an island off
the Gulf Coast of Florida. He wasn't exactly on a Midwinter
Conference. He'd quit going to those years before, after my
mother had died. But he was sharing a condo with a woman
friend who always overestimated the remedial powers of sexual
aerobics. Or maybe she only underestimated the progress of his
heart disease. We all knew it was coming. In the first year of his
widowhood, he sat in his chair, heartsore, waiting for the other
shoe to drop. Then he started going out with women. The
brothers were glad for him. The sisters rolled their eyes a lot. I
think they call these "gender issues." In the two years of consortium that followed, he'd had a major—which is to say a
chest ripping, down for the count—heart attack every six
months like clockwork. He survived all but one. "Three out of
four" I can hear him saying. "You're still dead when its over."
He'd had enough. Even now I think of that final scene in
David Lean's old film when Zhivago's heart is described as
"paper thin." He thinks he sees Lara turning a corner in
Moscow. He struggles to get off the bus, loosens his tie, finally
makes it to the sidewalk where, after two steps, he drops dead.
Dead chasing love, the thing we would die for. That was my
father—stepping not off a bus but out of a shower in his time-
share condo, not in Moscow but on Boca Grande, but chasing,
just as certainly, love. Chasing it to death.

When we got the call from his woman friend, we knew
what to do. My brother and I had done the drill in our heads
before. We had a travelling kit of embalming supplies: gloves,
fluids, needles, odds and ends. We had to explain to the security people at the airlines who scrutinized the contents of the
bag, wondering how we might make a bomb out of Dodge

Permaglo or overtake the cabin crew with a box marked "Slaughter Surgical Supplies" full of stainless steel oddities they'd never seen before. When we got to the funeral home they had taken him to, taken his body to, the undertaker there asked if we were sure we wanted to do this—our own father, after all?—he'd be happy to call in one of his own embalmers. We assured him it would be OK. He showed us into the prep room, that familiar decor of porcelain and tile and florescent light—a tidy scientific venue for the witless horror of mortality, for how easily we slip from is to isn't.

It was something we had always promised him, though I can't now, for the life of me, remember the context in which it was made—the promise that when he died his sons would embalm him, dress him, pick out a casket, lay him out, prepare the obits, contact the priests, manage the flowers, the casseroles, the wake and procession, the Mass and burial. Maybe it was just understood. His was a funeral he would not have to direct. It was ours to do; and though he'd directed thousands of them, he had never made mention of his own preferences. Whenever he was pressed on the matter he would only say, "You'll know what to do." We did.

There's this "just a shell" theory of how we ought to relate to dead bodies. You hear a lot of it from young clergy, old family friends, well-intentioned in-laws—folks who are unsettled by the fresh grief of others. You hear it when you bring a mother and a father in for the first sight of their dead daughter, killed in a car wreck or left out to rot by some mannish violence. It is proffered as comfort in the teeth of what is a comfortless situation, consolation to the inconsolable. Right between the inhale and exhale of the bonewracking sob such hurts produce, some frightened and well-meaning ignoramus is bound to give out with "It's OK, that's not her, it's just a shell." I once saw an Episcopalian deacon nearly decked by the swift slap of the mother of a teenager, dead of leukemia, to whom he'd tendered this counsel. "I'll tell you when *it's* 'just a shell,' " the woman said. "For now and until I tell you otherwise, *she's* my daughter." She was asserting the longstanding right of the living to declare the dead dead. Just as we declare the living alive through baptisms, lovers in love by nuptials, funerals are the way we close the gap between the death that happens and the death that matters. It's how we assign meaning to our little remarkable histories.

And the rituals we devise to conduct the living and beloved and the dead from one status to another have less to do with *performance* than with *meaning*. In a world where "dysfunctional" has become the operative adjective, a body that has ceased to work has, it would seem, few useful applications—its dysfunction more manifest than the sexual and familial forms that fill our tabloids and talk shows. But a body that doesn't work is, in the early going, the evidence we have of a person who has ceased to be. And a person who has ceased to be is as compelling a prospect as it was when the Neanderthal first dug holes for his dead, shaping the questions we still shape in the face of death: "Is that all there is?" "What does it mean?" "Why is it cold?" "Can it happen to me?"

So to suggest in the early going of grief that the dead body is "just" anything rings as tinny in its attempt to minimalize as it would if we were to say it was "just" a bad hair day when the girl went bald from her chemotherapy. Or that our hope for heaven on her behalf was based on the belief that Christ raised "just" a body from dead. What if, rather than crucifixion, he'd opted for suffering low self-esteem for the remission of sins? What if, rather than "just a shell," he'd raised his personality, say, or The Idea of Himself? Do you think they'd have changed the calendar for that? Done the Crusades? Burned witches? Easter was a body and blood thing, no symbols, no euphemisms, no half measures. If he'd raised anything less, of course, as Paul points out, the deacon and several others of us would be out of business or back to Saturday sabbaths, a sensible diet, and no more Christmases.

The bodies of the newly dead are not debris nor remnant, nor are they entirely icon or essence. They are, rather, changelings, incubates, hatchlings of a new reality that bear our names and dates, our image and likenesses, as surely in the eyes and ears of our children and grandchildren as did word of our birth in the ears of our parents and their parents. It is wise to treat such new things tenderly, carefully, with honor.

I had seen my father horizontal before. At the end it had been ICUs mostly, after his coronaries and bypasses. He'd been helpless, done unto. But before that there had been the man stretched out on the living room floor tossing one or the other of my younger siblings in the air; or napping in his office at the first funeral home in full uniform, black three-piece suit, striped tie, wingtips, clean shave; or in the bathtub singing "from the halls of Montezuma to the shores of Tripoli." He had outbreaks of the malaria he'd gotten in the South Pacific. In my childhood he was, like every father on the block, invincible. That he would die had been a fiction in my teens, a fear in my twenties, a specter in my thirties and, in my forties, a fact.

But seeing him, outstretched on the embalming table of the Anderson Mortuary in Ft. Myers with the cardiac blue in his ears and fingertips and along his distal regions, shoulders and lower ribs and buttocks and heels, I thought, *this is what my father will look like when he's dead.* And then, like a door slammed shut behind you, the tense of it all shifted into the inescapable present of *this is my father, dead.* My brother and I hugged each other, wept with each other and for each other and for our sisters and brothers home in Michigan. Then I kissed my father's forehead, not yet a shell. Then we went to work in the way our father had trained us.

He was a cooperative body. Despite the arteriosclerosis, his circulatory system made the embalming easy. And having just stepped from the shower into his doom, he was clean and cleanly shaven. He hadn't been sick, in the hospice or intensive care sense of the word. So there were none of the bruises on him or tubes in him that medical science can inflict and install. He'd gotten the death he wanted, caught in full stride, quick and cleanly after a day strolling the beach picking sea shells for the grandchildren and maybe after a little bone bouncing with his condo-mate, though she never said and we never asked and can only hope. And massaging his legs, his hands, his arms, to effect the proper distribution of fluid and drainage, watching the blue clear from his fingertips and heels as the fluid that would preserve him long enough for us to take our leave of him worked its way around his body, I had the sense that I was doing something for him even though, now dead, he was beyond my kindnesses or anyone's. Likewise, his body bore a kind of history: the tattoo with my mother's name on it he'd had done as an eighteen-year-old marine during World War II, the perfectly trimmed mustache I used to watch him darken with my mother's mascara when he was younger than I am and I was younger than my children are. The scars from his quintuple bypass surgery, the A.A. medallion he never removed, and the signet ring my mother gave him for his fortieth birthday, all of us saving money in a jar until fifty dollars was accumulated. Also there were the graying chest hairs, the hairless ankles, the male pattern baldness I see on the heads of men in the first-class section of airplanes and in the double mirrors in the barber's shop. Embalming my father I was reminded of how we bury our dead and then become them. In the end I had to say that maybe *this is what I'm going to look like dead*.

Maybe it was at a Midwinter Conference my father first thought about what he did and why he did it. He always told us that embalming got to be, forgive me, *de rigueur* during the Civil War when, for the first time in our history, lots of people— mostly men, mostly soldiers—were dying far from home and the families that grieved them. Dismal traders worked in tents on the edge of the battlefields charging, one reckons, what the traffic

would bear to disinfect, preserve, and "restore" dead bodies—
which is to say they closed mouths, sutured bullet holes, stitched
limbs or parts of limbs back on, and sent the dead back home to
wives and mothers, fathers and sons. All of this bother and
expense was predicated on the notion that the dead need to be at
their obsequies, or, more correctly, that the living need the dead
to be there, so that the living can consign them to the field or fire
after commending them to God or the gods or Whatever Is Out
There. The presence and participation of the dead human body
at its funeral is, as my father told it, every bit as important as the
bride's being at her wedding, the baby at its baptism.

And so we brought our dead man home. Flew his body
back, faxed the obits to the local papers, called the priests, the
sexton, the florists and stonecutter. We act out things we cannot put in words.

Back in '63, I can remember my father saying that the reason we have funerals and open caskets was so that we might
confront what he called "the reality of death." I think he'd
heard that at one of these conferences. Jessica Mitford had just
sold a million copies of *The American Way of Death*, Evelyn
Waugh had already weighed in with *The Loved One*, and talk
had turned at cocktail parties to "barbaric rituals" and "morbid
curiosities." The mortuary associations were scrambling for
some cover. Clergy and educators and psychologists—the new
clergy—were assembled to say it served some purpose, after all,
was emotionally efficient, psychologically correct, to do what
we'd been doing all along. The track record was pretty good
on this. We'd been doing—the species, not the undertakers—
more or less the same thing for millennia: looking up while
digging down, trying to make some sense of all of it, disposing
of our dead with sufficient pause to say they'd lived in ways
different from rocks and rhododendrons and even orangutans
and that those lives were worth mentioning and remembering.

Then Kennedy was shot dead and then Lee Harvey Oswald
and we spent the end of November that year burying them—

the first deaths in our lives that took for most of us boomers. All the other TV types got shot on *Gunsmoke* on a Friday and turned up on *Bonanza*, looking fit by Sunday night. But Kennedy was one of those realities of death my father must have been talking about and though we saw his casket and cortege and little John John saluting and the widow in her sunglasses, we never saw Kennedy dead, most of us, until years later when pictures of the autopsy were released and we all went off to the movies to see what really happened. In the interim, rumors circulated about Kennedy not being dead at all but hooked to some secret and expensive hardware, brainless but breathing. And when the Zapruder film convinced us that he must have died, still we lionized the man beyond belief. Of course, once we saw him dead in the pictures, his face, his body, he became human again: lovable and imperfect, memorable and dead.

And as I watch my generation labor to give their teenagers and young adults some "family values" between courses of pizza and Big Macs, I think maybe Gladstone had it right. I think my father did. They understood that the meaning of life is connected, inextricably, to the meaning of death; that mourning is a romance in reverse, and if you love, you grieve and there are no exceptions—only those who do it well and those who don't. And if death is regarded as an embarrassment or an inconvenience, if the dead are regarded as a nuisance from whom we seek a hurried riddance, then life and the living are in for like treatment. McFunerals, McFamilies, McMarriage, McValues. This is the mathematical precision the old Britisher was talking about and what my father was talking about when he said we'd know what to do.

Thus tending to his death, his dead body, had for me the same importance as being present for the births of my sons, my daughter. Some expert on *Oprah* might call this "healing." Another on

Donahue might say "cathartic." Over on *Geraldo* it might have "scarred him for life." And Sally Jesse Whatshername might mention "making good choices." As if they were talking about men who cut umbilical cords and change diapers or women who confront their self-esteem issues or their date rapists.

It is not about choices or functions or psychological correctness. A dead body has had its options limited, its choices narrowed. It is an old thing in the teeth of which we do what has been done because it is the thing to do. We needn't reinvent the wheel or make the case for it, though my generation always seems determined to.

And they are at it over on the other island. Trying to reinvent the funeral as "a vehicle for the healthy expression of grief," which, of course, it is; or as "a brief therapy for the acutely bereaved," which, of course, it is. There will be talk of "stages," "steps," "recovery." Someone will mention "aftercare," "post-funeral service follow-up," Widow to Widow programs, Mourners Anonymous? And in the afternoons they'll play nine holes, or go snorkeling or start cocktails too early and after dinner they'll go dancing then call home to check in with their offices just before they go to bed, to check on the gross sales, to see who among their townspeople has died.

Maybe I'll take the boat over tomorrow. Maybe some of the old timers are there—men of my father's generation, men you could call in the middle of the night if there was trouble. They remind me of my father and of Gladstone. Maybe they'll say I remind them of him.

Crapper

Death and the sun are not to be looked at in the face.

—La Rochefoucauld, *Maxims*

Don Paterson and I were crossing the Wolfe Tone Bridge in Galway contemplating Thomas Crapper. This was at early o'clock in the morning on our way back from an awful curry at the only Indian restaurant open in Galway in the wee hours. The night was mild, and our thoughts drifted toward talk of Crapper as the air behind us burned with the elemental fire of flatulence. It was an awful curry.

Why else would two internationally unknown poets, in Galway to recite our internationally unheard of poems, the guests of the Cuirt Festival of Literature, be talking about the implications of the invention of the flush toilet and about its inventor, that dismal man whose name shall forever be associated with shit? Why else?

Here, after all, was an opportunity to tender vengeance toward the man who'd damned, by faint praise, my most recent book of poems—in the *TLS* for chrissakes! Indeed, given Don's fairly damaged condition—a night of drink, the aforementioned curry—I could have pitched him headlong into the Corrib and watched him bob up and down out to Galway Bay humming like Bing Crosby, an odd and gaseous swan gone belly-up from bad food and good riddance. But really the review wasn't as bad as it was, well, "fair" and any ink is better than no ink, after all. And I like Don. He's an amiable Scot, a Dundonian, and a crackerjack poet if, like myself, not exactly a household name. It could be worse, I tell myself. We could be Crappers. And he still drinks well, in a way I never did, allowing excess to be its own reward—a little change from the tee-total life I live back in Michigan, where I haven't had a drink in years, suffering as I do from all of the "F" words: I'm fortyish, a father of four, a funeral director, and full of fear for what might happen if I go back on the Black Bush. So I don't.

The first time I was ever in Ireland was twenty-seven years ago. Driven by curiosity about my family and my affection for the poetry of William Butler Yeats—an internationally known poet—I saved up a hundred dollars beyond the cost of a one-way ticket and lit out, twenty and cocksure, for Ireland. Several of my generation were going off to Vietnam at the time but I'd drawn high numbers in the Nixon lotto so I was free to go. What made me so cocksure was the faith that my parents would bail me out if I got too deep into trouble. So I wasn't exactly like Kerouac or Woody Guthrie but I was, nonetheless, on the road. Or more precisely, flying the friendly skies.

When I located my cousins Tommy and Nora Lynch—brother and sister, bachelor and spinster—they lived in a thatched house on the west coast of Clare, in the townland of Moveen, with flagstone floors, two light sockets, a hot plate and open hearth, and no plumbing. Water existed five fields down the land, bubbling up in a miracle of springwater, clear and cold and clean. I soon learned to grab the bucket and a bit of the *Clare Champion* and on my way down for the precious water, I'd squat to my duties and wipe my ass with the obits or want ads or the local news. It was my first taste of Liberty—to crap out in the open air on the acreage of my ancestors, whilst listening to the sounds of morning: an aubade of birdwhistle and windsong.

Tommy and Nora kept cows, saved hay, went to the creamery and, as any farmer knows, dung is a large part of that bargain. It greens the grass that feeds the cow that makes the milk and shits again: a paradigm for the internal combustion engine, a closed system, efficient as an old Ford. And so the addition of my little bits of excrement to the vast dung-covered acreage was hardly noticeable, like personal grief among paid wailers, it gets lost in the shuffle and becomes anonymous and safe. This is the model for the food chain: the elements of feed, cowshit and what-have-ye, get lost in the shuffle by the time we sit down to the Delmonico or t-bone, likewise we are blind to the copulation of chickens and the habits of pigs when we sit down to the bacon and the eggs. The process blurs—dead fish make onions grow, manure turns into hamburger and tossed salad.

It was a good life. After nights of song and stories and poetry, common in the country in those years before televisions replaced the fire on the floor as the thing stared at and into, I would step out the back door of the cottage and take my stance amid the whitethorn trees my great-great-grandfather had planted years ago as saplings brought home from a horse fair in Kilrush. And looking up into the bright firmament I'd piss the porter out—I was young, I drank too much—and in the midst of this deliverance I'd look up into the vast firmament, as bright in its heaven as the dark was black, and think thoughts of Liberty and be thankful to be alive.

Years after, I would try to replicate these reveries when I found myself living in a large old house on Liberty Boulevard in a small town in Michigan. I lived next door to my funeral home and, returning in the early mornings from embalming one of my townspeople, I'd stop near the mock-orange tree by the back door of my home and look up into the heavens and relieve myself. Some nights I would espy Orion or the

Pleiades and think of mythologies blurred in my remembrance of them and be thankful for the life of the body and the mind.

Such was the firmament this night in Galway. Don and I had stood shoulder to shoulder before the famous green storefront of Kenny's Bookshop in High Street, swooning and stuporous to see our books, our faces, and bold notice of our readings there in the window among the stars. And despite the flatus, harbinger of impending disaster, Don and I were glad to be alive. Glad for the soft air of springtime, somehow sweeter in Galway than Dundee or Michigan. And glad to be paid for giving out with poems when so few can say they were ever paid for the inner workings of their souls. And glad, I daresay, for the rooms provided for us at the Atlanta Hotel in Dominick Street by the Festival Committee—rooms with solid beds and flush toilets toward which we made our gaseous ways that mild Marchy night in the City of the Tribes.

I still have the house in West Clare. Tommy died and Nora outlived him by twenty-one years, living alone by the fire. Then Nora died, just shy of her ninetieth birthday, a tidy jaundiced corpse, made little and green by pancreatic cancer. She left the house to me. I was her family. I kept coming back to West Clare after that first time, year after year, though the visits were shortened by the building of my business and the making of babies.

When her brother Tommy died, in 1971, she rode the bike into town and called from the post office. I flew over in time for the wake and funeral. I think that was when she began to count me as her next of kin—the one she could call and be sure I'd come. I think that's when she began to trust me with her own obsequies, mention of which was never made until the week before she died.

Of course, first among the several changes I made was the addition of a toilet and shower. I added on a room out the back door and put in a bathroom like a French bordello, all tile

and glowing fixtures. I had a septic tank sunk in the back hag-
gard and declared the place all the more habitable for the trouble. I let it to writers when I'm not there.

But for every luxury there is a loss. Just as the installation of
a phone when Nora was eighty cost her the excitement of letters coming up the road with John Willie McGrath, the post-
man on his bike, and the installation of a television when she
was eighty-five meant that her friends gave up their twisting
relations in favor of *Dallas* reruns, so the introduction of modern toiletry removed from Moveen forever the liberty of walking out into the night air or the morning mist with a full bowel
or bladder and having at the landscape in ways that can only be
called "close to nature."

The thing about the new toilet is that it removes the evidence
in such a hurry. The flush toilet, more than any single invention, has "civilized" us in a way that religion and law could
never accomplish. No more the morning office of the chamber pot or outhouse, where sights and sounds and odors
reminded us of the corruptibility of flesh. Since Crapper's mar-
velous invention, we need only pull the lever behind us and
the evidence disappears, a kind of rapture that removes the
nuisance. This dynamic is what the sociologist, Phillip Slater,
called "The Toilet Assumption," back in the seventies in a
book called *The Pursuit of Loneliness*. He was right: having lost
the regular necessity of dealing with unpleasantries, we have
lost the ability to do so when the need arises. And we have lost
the community well versed in these calamities. In short, when
shit happens, we feel alone.

It is the same with our dead. We are embarrassed by them
in the way that we are embarrassed by a toilet that overflows
the night that company comes. It is an emergency. We call the
plumber.

I sometimes think the only firms that put their names on what they do anymore are firms that make toilets and direct funerals. In both cases there seems to be an effort to sound trustworthy, stable, established, honest. Twyford's Adamant, Armitage Shanks, Moen & Moen, Kohler come to mind. Most other enterprises seem hidden behind some "assumed name" someone is "Doing Business As." Drugstores and real estate agents have given up the surnames of their owners for the more dodgy corporate identities of BuyRite or PayLess or Real Estate One. Doctors and lawyers have followed, taking in their shingles and putting out neon with murky identities and corporate cover. Drygoods and greengrocers, furniture merchants, saloons and restaurants—all gone now to malls and marts and supermarkets with meaningless or fictional monikers. But funeral homes and water-closets still stubbornly proclaim the name of the ones you'll be doing business with. Lynch & Sons is the name of ours. Is it ego or identity crisis? I sometimes ask myself.

The house I live in here on Liberty was built in 1880. It had no plumbing at first. It had a cistern in the cellar to collect rainwater and likely had a pump in the kitchen and an outhouse in the backyard surrounded by lilacs. Next to the kitchen was a birthing room where agreeable women of that age had their babies. It was next to the kitchen because, as everyone knows, the having of babies and the boiling of water were gerundives forever linked in the common wisdom of the day. And after the babies were born and showed good signs of living (no sure thing then—more than half of the deaths in 1900 were children under twelve), they were christened, often in a room up front, the priest or parson standing between the aunts and uncles and grandparents that populated the households of that era, where everybody looked liked the Waltons with their John-Boys and Susans and goodnight Grampaws. These were big families, made large by the lovemaking of parents before the mercy of birth control turned families into Mommy and Daddy and 2.34 Johnnies and Sues and the modern welfare state turned households into Mommy and babies and a phantom man—like the "bull brought in a suitcase" to dairy cows in West Clare.

The homes were large to house multiple births and generations. These were households in which, just as babies were being birthed, grandparents were aging upstairs with chicken soup and doctors' home visits until, alas, they died and were taken downstairs to the same room the babies were christened in to get what was called then, "laid out." Between the births and deaths were the courtships—sparkings and spoonings between boys and girls just barely out of their teens, overseen by a maiden aunt who traded her talents for childcare and housekeeping for her place in the household. The smitten young people would sit on a "love seat"—large enough to look into each other's eyes and hold hands, small enough to prevent them getting horizontal. The aunt would appear at strategic intervals to ask about lemonade, teas, room temperatures, the young man's family. Decorum was maintained. The children married, often in the same room—the room with large pocket doors drawn for privacy and access. The room in which grandparents were waked and new babies were baptized and love was proffered and contracted—the parlor.

Half a century, two world wars, and the New Deal later, homes got smaller and garages got bigger as we moved these big events out of the house. The emphasis shifted from stability to mobility. The architecture of the family and the homes they lived in changed forever by invention and intervention and by the niggling sense that such things didn't belong in the house. At the same time, the birthing room became the downstairs "bath"—emphasis upon the cleanly function of indoor plumbing. Births were managed in the sparkling wards of hospitals, or for real romance, on the way, in cars. A common fiction had some hapless civil servant or taxi man birthing a baby in the backseat of a squad car or Buick. The same backseat, it was often assumed, where the baby was invented—sparking and spooning under the supervision of Aunt Cecilia having given way to "parking" under the patrol of Officer Mahoney. Like most important things, courtship was done en route, in transit, on the lam, in a car. Retirees were deported to Sun City. Elders grew aged and sickly not upstairs in their own beds, but in a series of institutional venues: rest homes, nursing homes, hospital wards, sanitoria. Which is where they died: the chance, in 1960, of dying in your own bed: less than one in ten.

And having lived their lives and died their deaths outside the home, they were taken to be laid out, not in the family parlor but to the *funeral* parlor, where the building was outfitted to look like the family parlors gone forever, busy with overstuffed furniture, fern stands, knickknacks, draperies, and the dead.

This is how my business came to be.

Just about the time we were bringing the making of water and the movement of bowels into the house, we were pushing the birthing and marriage and sickness and dying out. And if the family that prayed together stayed together in accordance with the churchy bromide, the one that shits together rarely sticks together.

We have no parlors anymore, no hearthsides. We have, rather, our family rooms in which light flickers from the widescreen multichannel TV on which we watch reruns of a life we are not familiar with. Kitchens are not cooked in, dining rooms go dusty. Living rooms are a kind of mausolea reserved for "company" that seldom comes. Lovemaking is done on those "getaway" weekends at the Hyatt or the Holidome. New homes are built with fewer bedrooms and more full baths. (Note how a half bath is not called a whole crapper.) And everyone has their "personal space," their privacy. The babies are in daycare, the elders are in Arizona or Florida or a nursing home with people their own age, and mom and dad are busting ass to pay for their "dream house" or the remodeled "master suite" where nothing much happens anymore of any consequence.

This is also why the funerals held in my funeral parlor lack an essential manifest—the connection of the baby born to the marriage made to the deaths we grieve in the life of a family. I have no weddings or baptisms in the funeral home and the folks that pay me have maybe lost sight of the obvious connections between the life and the death of us. And how the rituals by which we mark the things that only happen to us once, birth and death, or maybe twice in the case of marriage, carry the same emotional mail—a message of loss and gain, love and grief, things changed utterly.

And just as bringing the crapper indoors has made feces an embarrassment, pushing the dead and dying out has made death one. Often I am asked to deal with the late uncle in the same way that Don Paterson and I were about to ask Armitage Shanks to deal with the bad curry—out of sight out of mind. Make it go away, disappear. Push the button, pull the chain, get on with life. The trouble is, of course, that life, as any fifteen-year-old can tell you, is full of shit and has but one death. And to ignore our excrement might be good form, while to ignore our mortality creates an "imbalance," a kind of spiritual irregularity, psychic impaction, a bunging up of our humanity, a denial of our very nature.

When Nora Lynch got sick they called. The doctor at the hospital in Ennis mentioned weeks, a month at most, there might be pain. I landed in Shannon on Ash Wednesday morning and on the way to the hospital stopped at the Cathedral in Ennis where school children and townies were getting their ashes before going off to their duties. The nurses at the hospi-

tal said I was holier than any one of them—to have flown over
and gotten the smudge on my forehead and it not 9 A.M. yet
in West Clare. Nora was happy to see me. I asked her what she
thought we ought to do. She said she wanted to go home to
Moveen. I told her the doctors all thought she was dying.
"What harm . . .," says she. "Aren't we all?" She fixed her
bright eyes on the spot in my forehead. I asked the doctors for
a day to make arrangements for her homecoming—a visiting
nurse from the county health office would make daily calls, the
local medico would manage pain with morphine, I laid in
some soups and porridges and ice creams, some adult diapers,
a portable commode.

The next day I drove back to Ennis to get her, buckled her
into the front seat of the rental car, and made for the west along
the same road I'd been driving toward her all those years since
my first landing in Shannon—an hour from Ennis to Kilrush to
Kilkee then five miles out the coast road to Moveen, the townland narrowing between the River Shannon's mouth and
North Atlantic, on the westernmost peninsula of County Clare.
It was the second day of Lent in Ireland, the green returning to
the fields wracked by winter, the morning teetering between
showers and sunlight. And all the way home on the road she
sang, "The Cliffs of Moveen," "The Rose of Tralee," "The
Boys of Kilmichael," "Amazing Grace."

"Nora," I said to her between verses, "no one would know
you are dying to hear you singing now."

"Whatever happens," she said, "I'm going home."

She was dead before Easter. Those last days spent by the fire
in ever shortening audiences with neighbors and priests and
Ann Murray, a neighbor woman I hired to "attend" her when
I wasn't there. Two powerful unmarried women, sixty years
between them, talking farming and missed chances, unwilling
to have their lives defined for them by men. Or deaths.

And I noticed how she stopped eating at all and wondered what the reason for that was.

When I first was in Ireland, that winter and spring a quarter century ago, Nora and I bicycled down to the Regan's farm in Donoughby. Mrs. Regan had had a heart attack We were vaguely related. We'd have to go. The body was laid out in her bedroom, mass cards strewn at the foot of the bed. Candles were lit. Holy water shook. Women knelt in the room saying rosaries. Men stood out in the yard talking prices, weather, smoking cigarettes. A young Yank, I was consigned to the women. In the room where Mrs. Regan's body was, despite the candles and the flowers and the February chill—a good thing in townlands where no embalming is done—there was the terrible odor of gastrointestinal distress. Beneath the fine linens, Mrs. Regan's belly seemed bulbous, almost pregnant, almost growing. Between decades of the rosary, neighbor women shot anxious glances among one another. Later I heard, in the hushed din of gossip, that Mrs. Regan, a light-hearted woman unopposed to parties, had made her dinner the day before on boiled cabbage and onions and ham and later followed with several half-pints of lager at Hickie's in Kilkee. And these forgivable excesses, while they may not have caused her death, were directly responsible for the heavy air inside the room she was waked in and the "bad form" Nora called it when the requiems had to be moved up a day and a perfectly enjoyable wake foreshortened by the misbehavior of Mrs. Regan's body.

At night Nora would crawl into bed, take the medicine for pain, and sleep. "Collins is our man," she told me toward the end, meaning the undertaker in Carrigaholt who could be counted on for coffins and hearses and grave openings at Moyarta where all our people were, back to our common man, Patrick Lynch. She turned over the bankbook with my name on it, added, she said, after her brother had died all those years ago. "Be sure there's plenty of sandwiches and porter and wine, sherry wine, something sweet. And whiskey for the ones that dig the grave."

Nora Lynch was a tidy corpse, quiet and continent, only a little jaundiced, which never showed in the half light of the room she died in, the room she was born in, the room she was waked in. She never stirred. And we waked her for three full days and nights in late March before taking her to church in Carrigaholt. Then buried her on a Monday in the same vaulted grave as her father and her father's father and her twin brother, dead in infancy, near ninety years before. We gave whiskey to the gravediggers and had a stone cut with her name and dates on it to overlook her grave and the River Shannon.

There was money enough for all of that. She'd saved. Enough for the priests and the best coffin Collins had and for pipers and tinwhistlers and something for the choir; and to take the entourage to the Long Dock afterward and fill them with food and stout and trade memories and tunes. It was a grand wake and funeral. We wept and laughed and sang and wept some more.

And afterward there was enough left over to build the room that housed the toilet and the shower and haul that ancient cottage—a wedding gift to my great-great grandfather, my inheritance—into the twentieth century in the nick of time.

Still, there are nights now in West Clare and nights in Michigan when I eschew the porcelain and plumbing in favor of the dark comforts of the yard, the whitethorn or lilac or the mock-orange, the stars in their heaven, the liberty of it; and the drift my thoughts invariably take toward the dead and the living and the ones I love whenever I am at the duties of my toilet.

I think of Nora Lynch and of Mrs. Regan and of the blessings of their lives among us. And lately I've been thinking thoughts of Don Paterson who made it back to the Atlanta Hotel—he to his room and me to mine. And maybe it was the drink or curry or the talk of toilets, or all of it together that made him kneel and hug the bowl and look into the maelstrom as we all have once or more than once, adding to the list of things not to be looked at in the face, the godawful name of Crapper.

The Right Hand of the Father

I had an uneventful childhood. Added to my mother's conviction that her children were precious was my father's terrible wariness. He saw peril in everything, disaster was ever at hand. Some mayhem with our name on it lurked around the edges of our neighborhood waiting for a lapse of parental oversight to spirit us away. In the most innocent of enterprises, he saw danger. In every football game he saw the ruptured spleen, the death by drowning in every backyard pool, leukemia in every bruise, broken necks on trampolines, the deadly pox or fever in every rash or bug bite.

It was, of course, the undertaking.

As a funeral director, he was accustomed to random and unreasonable damage. He had learned to fear.

My mother left big things to God. Of her nine children, she was fond of informing us, she had only "planned" one. The rest of us, though not entirely a surprise—she knew what caused it—were gifts from God to be treated accordingly. Likewise, she figured on God's protection and, I firmly believe, she believed in the assignment of guardian angels whose job it was to keep us all out of harm's way.

But my father had seen, in the dead bodies of infants and children and young men and women, evidence that God lived by the Laws of Nature, and obeyed its statutes, however brutal. Kids died of gravity and physics and biology and natural selection. Car wrecks and measles and knives stuck in toasters, household poisons, guns left loaded, kidnappers, serial killers, burst appendices, bee stings, hard-candy chokings, croups untreated—he'd seen too many instances of His unwillingness to overrule the natural order, which included, along with hurricanes and meteorites and other Acts of God, the aberrant disasters of childhood.

So whenever I or one of my siblings would ask to go here or there or do this or that, my father's first response was almost always "No!" He had just buried someone doing that very thing.

He had just buried some boy who had toyed with matches, or played baseball without a helmet on, or went fishing without a life preserver, or ate the candy that a stranger gave him. And what the boys did that led to their fatalities matured as my brothers and sisters and I matured, the causes of their death becoming subtly interpersonal rather than cataclysmic as we aged. The stories of children struck by lightning were replaced by narratives of unrequited love gone suicidal, teenagers killed by speed and drink or overdosed on drugs, and hordes of the careless but otherwise blameless dead who'd found themselves *in the wrong place at the wrong time.*

My mother, who had more faith in the power of prayer and her own careful parenting, would often override his prohibitions. "Oh, Ed," she would argue over dinner, "Leave them be! They've got to learn some things for themselves." Once she told him "Don't be ridiculous, Ed," when he'd refused me permission to spend the night at a friend's house across the street. "What!" she scolded him, "Did you just bury someone who died of a night spent at Jimmy Shryock's house?"

He regarded my mother's interventions not as contrarieties, but as the voice of reason in a world gone mad. It was simply the occasional triumph of her faith over his fear. And when she stepped into the fray with her powerful testimony, he reacted as the drunken man does to the cold water and hot coffee, as if to say, *Thanks, I needed that.*

But his fear was genuine and not unfounded. Even for suburban children who were loved, wanted, protected, doted over, there were no guarantees. The neighborhood was infested with rabid dogs, malarial mosquitoes, weirdoes disguised as mailmen and teachers. The worst seemed always on the brink of happening, as his daily rounds informed him. For my father, even the butterflies were suspect.

So while my mother said her prayers and slept the sound sleep of a child of God; my father was ever wakeful, ever vigilant, ever in earshot of a phone—in case the funeral home should call in the middle of the night—and a radio that monitored police and fire calls. In my childhood I can recall no day he was not up and waiting for me and my siblings to awaken. Nor can I remember any night I lived at home, until I was nineteen, when he was not awake and waiting for our arrival home.

Every morning brought fresh news of overnight catastrophes he'd heard on the radio. And every night brought stories of the obsequies, sad and deliberate, which he directed. Our breakfasts and dinners were populated by the widowed and heartsore, the wretched and bereft, among them the parents permanently damaged by the death of a child. My mother would roll her eyes a little bit and dole out liberties against his worry. Eventually we were allowed to play hardball, go camping, fish alone, drive cars, date, ski, open checking accounts, and run the other ordinary developmental risks—her faith moving mountains his fear created.

"Let go," she would say. "Let God."

Once she even successfully argued on behalf of my older brother, Dan, getting a BBGun, a weapon which he promptly turned against his younger siblings, outfitting us in helmet and leather jacket and instructing us to run across Eaton Park while he practiced his marksmanship. Today he is a colonel in the army and the rest of us are gun-shy.

Far from indifferent, my mother left the business of Life and Death to God in His heaven. This freed her to tend to the day-to-day concerns of making sure we lived up to our potential. She was concerned with "character," "integrity," "our contribution to society," and "the salvation of our souls." She made no secret of her belief that God would hold her personally accountable for the souls of her children—a radical notion today—so that her heaven depended on our good conduct.

For my father, what we did, who we became, were incidental to the tenuous fact of our being: That We Were seemed sufficient for the poor worried man. The rest, he would say, was gravy.

There were, of course, near misses. After the usual flues, poxes, and measles, we entered our teen years in the sixties and seventies. Pat was sucker-punched in a bar fight by a man who broke a beer bottle over his head. Eddie drove off a bridge, crashed his car into the riverbank, and walked away unscathed. He told our parents that another car, apparently driven by an intoxicant, had run him off the road. We called it "Eddie's Chappaquiddick" privy as only siblings are to our brother's taste for beer and cocaine. Julie Ann went through the windshield of a friend's car when the friend drove into a tree and, except for some scalpline lacerations and scars, lived to tell about it. Brigid took too many pills one night in combination with strong drink and what her motivation was remained a mystery for years, known only to my mother. For my part, I fell off a third-story fire-escape in my third year of college, broke several Latin-sounding bones, fractured my pelvis, and compressed three vertebrae but never lost consciousness. My English professor and mentor, the poet Michael Heffernan, was first downstairs and out the door to where I had landed. I must have appeared somewhat dazed and breathless. "Did you hit your head?" he kept asking once he had determined I was alive. "What day is it?" "Who is the president of the United States?" To assure him I had not suffered brain damage, I gave out with "The Love Song of J. Alfred Prufrock"—a moving rendition I was later told, marred only by my belching through the couplet where your man says, "I grow old . . . I grow old . . . I shall wear the bottoms of my trousers rolled." Then I puked, not from the fall but from the J.W. Dant Bourbon that was credited with saving my life. I had been sufficiently limbered up, it was reasoned, by generous doses of Kentucky sour mash, to have avoided permanent damage.

In the hospital I woke to a look on my father's face I shall always remember—a visage distorted by rage and relief, at war with itself. And by amazement at the menagerie of friends and fellow revelers who accompanied me to hospital. While Professor Heffernan could affect the upright citizen in tweeds and buttondowns, not so Walt Houston, who studied physics and comparative religion and lived most of the school year in a tree somewhere on the edge of the campus and scavenged for food scraps in the student union. Nor Myles Lorentzen, who successfully failed his draft physical after the ingestion of massive doses of caffeine—pot after pot of black coffee followed by the eating whole of a carton of cigarettes. Later, Myles would do hard time in prison for the illegal possession of marijuana. A month after his release they made possession a misdemeanor, punishable by a twenty dollar fine. Worse still, Glenn Wilson, whose only utterance after a six pack of beer was always "Far out, man!" which he would say, for no apparent reason, at the most inappropriate of times. Harmless drunks and ne'er-do-wells, my father looked suspicious of my choice of friends.

My mother thanked God I had not been killed, then fixed her eyes on me in a way it seemed she'd had some practice at—casting the cold eye of the long suffering in the face of a boozy loved one. My father had quit drinking the year before, joined A.A., began going to meetings. My brothers and I had been a little surprised by this as we had never seen him drunk before. I had overheard my mother's sister once, complaining aloud about my father's drinking. I must have been six or eight years old. I marched down to Aunt Pat's on the next block and told her out-right that my father wasn't a drunk. And once, the Christmas after his father had died, I heard him and my mother come home late. He was raving a little. I thought it must be grief. He insisted the doctor be called. He said he was having a heart attack. The doctor, I think, tried to cover for him, behaved as if there was something wrong other than drink. In any case, by the time I'd taken my dive off the balcony, my father had a year's sobriety under his belt and should have been able to recognize an inebriate when he saw one. But instead of a curse, he saw blessing: his son, somewhat broken but reparable and *alive*.

Now they are both dead and I reckon a fixture in my father's heaven is the absence of any of his children there, and a fixture in my mother's is the intuition that we will all follow, sooner or later but certainly.

We parent the way we were parented. The year they began to make real sense to me was 1974. In February the first of my children was born. In June we purchased the funeral home in Milford. I was a new parent and the new undertaker in a town where births and deaths are noticed. And one of the things I noticed was the number of stillbirths and fetal deaths we were called upon to handle. There was no nearby hospital twenty years ago; no medical office buildings around town. The prenatal care was not what it should be, and in addition to the hundred adult funerals we handled every year in those days, we would be called upon to take care of the burial of maybe a dozen infants—babies born dead, or born living but soon dead from some anomaly, and several every year from what used to be called crib death and is now called Sudden Infant Death Syndrome.

I would sit with the moms and dads of these babies—dead of no discernible cause—they simply forgot to breathe, trying to make some sense of all of it. The fathers, used to protecting and paying, felt helpless. The mothers seemed to carry a pain in their innards that made them appear breakable. The overwhelming message on their faces was that nothing mattered anymore, nothing. We would arrange little wakes and graveside services, order in the tiny caskets with the reversible interiors of pink and blue, dust off the "baby bier" on which the casket would rest during the visitation, and shrink all the customs and accouterments to fit this hurt.

When we bury the old, we bury the known past, the past we imagine sometimes better than it was, but the past all the same, a portion of which we inhabited. Memory is the overwhelming theme, the eventual comfort.

But burying infants, we bury the future, unwieldy and unknown, full of promise and possibilities, outcomes punctuated by our rosy hopes. The grief has no borders, no limits, no known ends, and the little infant graves that edge the corners and fencerows of every cemetery are never quite big enough to contain that grief. Some sadnesses are permanent. Dead babies do not give us memories. They give us dreams.

And I remember in those first years as a father and a funeral director, new at making babies and at burying them, I would often wake in the middle of the night, sneak into the rooms where my sons and daughter slept, and bend to their cribsides to hear them breathe. It was enough. I did not need astronauts or presidents or doctors or lawyers. I only wanted them to breathe. Like my father, I had learned to fear.

And, as my children grew, so too the bodies of dead boys and girls I was called upon to bury—infants becoming toddlers, toddlers becoming school children, children becoming adolescents, then teens, then young adults, whose parents I would know from the Little League or Brownies or PTA or Rotary or Chamber of Commerce. Because I would not keep in stock an inventory of children's caskets, I'd order them, as the need arose, in sizes and half sizes from two foot to five foot six, often estimating the size of a dead child, not yet released from the county morgue, by the sizes of my own children, safe and thriving and alive. And the caskets I ordered were invariably "purity and gold" with angels on the corners and shirred crepe interiors of powdery pink or baby blue. And I would never charge more than the wholesale cost of the casket and throw in our services free of charge with the hope in my heart that God would, in turn, spare me the hollowing grief of these parents.

There were exceptions to the "purity and gold." Once a man whose name I remember shot his two children, ages eight and four, while their mother waited tables up in town. Then he shot himself. We laid him out in an 18-gauge steel with the Last Supper on the handles and his daughter and his son in a matching casket together. The bill was never paid. She sold the house, skipped town. I never pursued it.

And one Christmastide twin six-year-olds fell through the ice on the river that divides this town. It ran through their backyard and no one knows if they went in together or one tried to save the other. But the first of the brothers was found the same day and the next one was found two days later, bobbed up downstream after the firemen broke up the ice by the dam. We put them in the one casket with two pillows, foot to foot—identical in their new Oshkosh B'Gosh jeans and plaid shirts their mother had mail-ordered from Sears for Christmas. Their father, a young man then, aged overnight and died within five years of nothing so much as sorrow. Their mother got cancer and died after that of grief metastasized. The only one left, the twins' older brother, who must be nearing thirty now, is long gone from this place.

And I remember the poor man with the look of damage on him whose wife strangled their eight-year-old son with a belt. Then she wrote a fourteen-page suicide note, explaining why she felt her son, who had been slow to read, faced a lifetime of ridicule and failure she felt she was freeing him from. Then she took three dozen pills, lay down beside the boy, and died herself. First he selected a cherry casket and laid them out together in it, the boy at rest under his mother's arm. But before the burial, he asked to have the boy removed from the mother's casket and placed in one of his own and buried in his own grave. I did as he instructed and thought it was sensible.

So early on I learned my father's fear. I saw in every move my children made the potentially lethal outcome. We lived in an old house next door to the funeral home. The children grew up playing football in the side yard, roller skating in the parking lot, then skateboarding, riding bikes, then driving cars. When they were ten, nine, six, and four, their mother and I divorced. She moved away. I was "awarded" custody—four badly saddened kids I felt a failure towards. And though I was generally pleased with the riddance that divorce provides—the marriage had become a painful case—I was suddenly aware that single parenting meant, among other things, one pair of eyes to watch out for one's children with. Not two. One pair of ears to keep to the ground. One body to place between them and peril; one mind. There was less conflict and more worry. The house itself was dangerous: poison under every sink, electrocution in every appliance, radon in the basement, contagion in the kitty litter. Having been proclaimed by the courts the more "fit" parent, I was determined to be one.

I would rise early, make the sack lunches while they ate cereal, then drive them to school. I had a housekeeper who came at noon to do the laundry and clean and be there when the youngest came home from kindergarten. I'd be at the office from nine-thirty until four o'clock, then come home to get dinner ready—stews mostly, pastas, chicken and rice. They never ate as much as I prepared. Then there was homework and dance classes and baseball, then bed. And when it was done, when they were in bed and the house was ahum with its appliances, washer and dryer and dishwasher and stereo, I'd pour myself a tumbler of Irish whiskey, sit in a wingback chair and smoke and drink and listen—on guard for whatever it was that would happen next.

Most nights I passed out in the chair, from fatigue or whiskey or from both. I'd crawl up to bed, sleep fitfully, and rise early again.

The poor cousin of fear is anger.

It is the rage that rises in us when our children do not look both ways before running into busy streets. Or take to heart the free advice we're always serving up to keep them from pitfalls and problems. It is the spanking or tongue lashing, the door slammed, the kicked dog, the clenched fist—the love, Godhelpus, that hurts: the grief. It is the war we wage against those facts of life over which we have no power, none at all. It makes for heroes and histrionics but it is no way to raise children.

And there were mornings I'd awaken heroic and angry, hungover and enraged at the uncontrollable facts of my life: the constant demands of my business, the loneliness of my bed, the damaged goods my children seemed. And though it was anything but them I was really angry at, it was the kids who'd get it three mornings out of every five. I never hit, thank God, or screamed. The words were measured out, meticulous. I seethed. After which I would apologize, pad their allowances, and curry forgiveness the way any drunk does with the ones he loves. Then I stopped drinking, and while the fear did not leave entirely, the anger subsided. I was not "in recovery" so much as I was a drunk who didn't drink and eventually came to understand that I was more grateful than resentful for the deliverance.

But faith is, so far as I know it, the only known cure for fear—the sense that someone is in charge here, is checking the ID's and watching the borders. Faith is what my mother said: letting go and letting God—a leap into the unknown where we are not in control but always welcome. Some days it seems like stating the obvious. Some days it feels like we are entirely alone.

Here is a thing that happened. I just buried a young girl whose name was Stephanie, named for St. Stephen; the patron of stonemasons, the first martyr. She died when she was struck by a cemetery marker as she slept in the back seat of her parents' van as the family was driving down the interstate on their way to Georgia. It was the middle of the night. The family had left Michigan that evening to drive to a farm in Georgia where the Blessed Mother was said to appear and speak to the faithful on the thirteenth of every month. As they motored down the highway in the dark through mid-Kentucky, some local boys, half an hour south, were tipping headstones in the local cemetery for something to do. They picked one up that weighed about fourteen pounds—a stone. What they wanted with it is anyone's guess. And as they walked across the overpass of the interstate, they grew tired of carrying their trophy. With not so much malice as mischief, they tossed it over the rail as the lights of southbound traffic blurred below them. It was at this moment that the van that Stephanie's father was driving intersected with the stolen marker from the local cemetery. The stone was falling earthward at thirty-two feet per second, per second. The van was heading south at seventy miles per hour. The stone shattered the windshield, glanced off Stephanie's father's right shoulder, woke her mother riding in the passenger seat and, parting the space between the two front seats, struck Stephanie in the chest as she lay sleeping in the back seat. She had just traded places with her younger brother who cuddled with his two other sisters in the rear seat of the van. It did not kill Stephanie instantly. Her sternum was broken, her heart bruised beyond repair. A trucker stopped to radio for help but at two A.M. in Nowhere, Kentucky, on a Friday morning, such things take time. The family waited by the roadside reciting the rosary as Stephanie gasped for air and moaned. They declared her dead at the hospital two hours later. Stephanie's mother found the stone in the back seat and gave it to the authorities. It said RESERVED FOSTER and was reckoned to be a corner marker from the Foster Lot in Resurrection Cemetery.

Sometimes it seems like multiple choice.

A: It was the Hand of God. God woke up one Friday the 13th and said, "I want Stephanie!" How else to explain the fatal intersection of bizarre events. Say the facts slowly, they sound like God's handiwork. If the outcome were different, we'd call it a miracle.

Or *B*: It wasn't the Hand of God. God knew it, got word of it sooner or later, but didn't lift a hand because He knows how much we've come to count on the Laws of Nature—gravity and objects in motion and at rest—so He doesn't fiddle with the random or deliberate outcomes. He regrets to inform us of this, but surely we must understand His position.

Or *C*: The Devil did it. If faith supports the existence of Goodness, then it supports the probability of Evil. And sometimes, Evil gets the jump on us.

Or *D*: None of the above. Shit happens. That's Life, get over it, get on with it.

Or maybe *E*: All of the above. Mysteries—like decades of the rosary—glorious and sorrowful mysteries.

Each of the answers leaves my inheritance intact—my father's fear, my mother's faith. If God's will, shame on God is what I say. If not, then shame on God. It sounds the same. I keep shaking a fist at the Almighty asking *Where were you on the morning of the thirteenth?* The alibi changes every day.

Of course the answers, the ones that faith does not require, and are not forthcoming, would belong to Stephanie's parents and the hundreds I've known like them over the years.

I've promised Stephanie's headstone by Christmas—actually for St. Stephen's Day, December 26th. The day we all remember singing Good King Wenceslaus. Stephen was accused of blasphemy and stoned in 35 A.D.

When I first took Stephanie's parents to the cemetery, to buy a grave for their daughter, her mother stood in the road and pointed to a statue of The Risen Christ. "I want her over there," she said, "at the right hand of Jesus." We walked across the section to an empty, unmarked space underneath the outstretched granite right arm of Christ. "Here," Stephanie's mother said, her wet eyes cast upward into the gray eyes of Christ. Stephanie's father, his eyes growing narrow, was reading the name on the neighboring grave. FOSTER is what it read. It was cut in stone.

Words Made Flesh

Events unfold in ways that make us think of God. They achieve, in their happening, a symmetry and order that would be frightening if assigned to Chance. Things that happen here intersect with things that happen elsewhere, as if there were a plan. Coincidence makes way for correlation which, in its turn, bespeaks the intimate consortium of cause and effect—first in whispers, then in the full blushless voice of certainty: *because* it says, *because*. Eventually everything is suspect: I wash the car, it rains; she wears that perfume, he is dizzy with desire; as long as you whistle that tune no tigers appear. Ironies? Happenstance? Or is it that tune that keeps the tigers at bay? The finger of fate or of fate's Maker that taps, deliberately, those dominoes, the tipping of which, down the ages, is history.

Two years ago, my friend and mentor, the poet Henry Nugent, was cast into woe by the sudden dissolution of his second marriage. In hindsight there are always signs: troubles with teenagers, the death of elderly parents, professional appointments and disappointments. To the imponderable crises of middle age were added the ordinary stresses on a marriage that had survived seventeen years but would not make another.

They had met when she was a student and he was an associate professor of English at a small state university in southeastern Kentucky. His first marriage, a barren, seven-year mismatch born of lust and mistrusting, had just been abandoned, amicably, as they say, before the accumulation of property or progeny. Henry Nugent, at thirty, had boyish good looks, a tenure-track position, no discernible emotional baggage, and a down payment on his literary estate in the form of his first book of poems on the shelf. Just out of her teens, the now former Mrs. Nugent was a singular beauty, darkly Italian, possessed of a marketable degree, her own ambitions, and the circumspection with respect to men you see in women raised with brothers. Hers were attributes of body and mind that amounted to more than the sum of those parts, which Henry spent the best part of the next two decades trying to decipher in verse. And she was attracted to the balance, she saw him always trying to maintain, between the tweedy man of letters and the lyric and irrepressible poet. That he made the whiteness of her inner thighs, the dark line of hairlets beneath her navel, and the bend of her body as she lay beside him the subject of well-crafted sonnets and villanelles and sestinas had been attractive in those early years. But if women in their twenties will trade favor for poems and warm to the easy duty of muses, by thirty they grow wary and by forty regard it as invasion of privacy and politically incorrect. They won't be muses. They've their own version of the story. But she was twenty then.

They were smitten. They married. Moved to Ohio. Made babies. And seemed happy enough until, on the brink of her thirty-seventh year, she called me one day to say she had had enough. She just needed a break. She couldn't take it any more. She took the boys and the Buick and drove back to Kentucky, only returning when he had been served with papers and evicted by a force of law and custom too many men in the Western world are familiar with.

Later, of course, the unflattering details shook out: a fling with a middle management type at the chicken processing plant.

The name brand of the chicken would be recognizable to frequenters of the fresh meats section of their local grocery. There were hushed references to "diagnoses," "appetites," and "tendencies." And public talk, inevitably, of the most private matters—trusts broken, faiths breached, a house divided by hurts. In the end it was a sadness, as all such events are sadnesses, beyond the consolation of friends or the power of prayer. It was a bad thing that happened to good, if not especially perfect, people.

If Love and Death are the great themes, the death of love, in the lives of poets, is a predictable mystery.

My friend, cut loose from the dockage of his household, looked into the barrel of his forty-seventh year bereft of wife and sons, bereft of the four-bedroom split-level he'd recently remortgaged, bereft of prospects of any kind. He came to the unhappy conclusion that many divorcing men with good life insurance come to—that the best thing he could do for his family, what was left of it, was to drop dead. His lawyer advised against rash judgments.

Halfway through the legal imbroglio, his fourth collection, *Good Counsel*, was published by a highly respected university press. It was dedicated to his soon to be former spouse, who couldn't have cared less, and to his sons, themselves not terribly impressed, lost as they were in the shuffle of marital failure. A brief but enthusiastic review in the *Washington Post* did little to cheer him, though it helped to sell, in one weekend, half of his book's first printing. Harried and hapless, he spent months immersed in the minutiae of divorce: attorneys, private investigators, depositions, interrogatories. A scholar by training and disposition, and a pushover for languages and jargon, he became conversant in case law and precedent, show-cause, suit and countersuit. When he once referred to his sons as "the minor children," I objected. I could not bear to hear these beautiful boys who had their mother's wisdom and their father's brains, his dark humor and her brown eyes, called anything but precious. He kept crafting his testimony and his closing arguments for a day in court I told him would never come. The billable hours on both sides were plentiful.

Once the litigants had spent all they had saved toward the boys' college educations, the attorneys, well paid for the rattling of sabers and the launching of salvos, met over sushi, divided the spoils, and agreed to meet for golf the following weekend, weather and caseloads permitting.

It was done.

Good counsel, near as anyone could figure, was unequivocally and irrevocably, finished.

On the grand scale of things, a sad man, adrift in south-central Ohio, compares unimportantly to the larger sorrows. War rages in the usual places, hunger whittles through whole populations. Plagues decimate the culture and the sub-cultures. The poor are with us always. The dead are everywhere. In such a world it is hard to work up sympathy for a white man with tenure, the lion's share of his pension left, visitation rights, his health, his job.

Heartbreak is an invisible affliction. No limp comes with it, no evident scar. No sticker is issued that guarantees good parking or easy access. The heart is broken all the same. The soul festers. The wound, untreated, can be terminal.

But in a world that distributes victim status like coin of the realm, my friend's demographics disqualified him from the institutional forms of relief. Where divorcing women are seen as taking charge of their lives, or getting out of abusive relationships, divorcing men are seen as damaged goods, deadbeat dads. Heartache is their comeuppance.

Truth told, he was hardly alone. Look closely on Saturdays and Sundays when the fast food places and the cinemas and malls fill up with the non-custodial parents doing their "quality time" with their children. Real parents stay home on weekends to garden or golf or watch old movies with slow stews simmering on the stove. But non-custodials live a different life: uprooted, on the lam, forced to fit a week's affection and discipline and guidance into what the losing attorney always calls their "liberal visitation rights." They have to hustle to get some semblance of home life with their children. Taco Bell takes the place of turkey and mashed potatoes. The mall replaces the Main Streets of home towns always described as a great place to raise the kids. Weeklong parents buy their children underwear and orthodontics. Weekenders buy them toys and talk of trips to Disney World in the sparkling future. Many give up trying, telling themselves it's too hard on the children, too hard on themselves. Too hard.

At first, both of the Nugents were calling me weekly, daily sometimes, sometimes twice a day. I reckoned I owed them both. Both of them had been willing to listen to me ten years before when my own ruined marriage was unraveling. So I listened back, tendered free advice, along with the disclaimer that you get what you pay for. She stopped calling when I broached the topic of conciliation. She wanted no part of that. But he kept calling. He was angry, heartwracked, crazy with love and hate. I was not always sympathetic. I felt as I supposed their boys did: divided and confused, utterly powerless. And oddly at risk since divorce has, like romance and suicide, its own contagion.

As these miseries were unfolding in Ohio, my friend and editor, the poet Robin Robertson, was tidying up loose ends in his office at Jonathan Cape Publishers in London. He had applied for and been granted a month-long residency at Annaghmakerrig, the Tyrone Guthrie Centre for the Arts in Newbliss, Co. Monaghan. His usual duties of publishing the novels and slim volumes of other writers was to be suspended while he prepared his own first manuscript for publication.

It was June in Newbliss. The rhododendron that surround the mansion were ablaze with blooms. Bernard Loughlin, the resident director, was working as always in the formal gardens. To the roses and other perennials, a few rows of bell-peppers, aubergine, tomatoes, and artichoke had been added. Robin Robertson sat at the desk in the bay window of Tyrone Guthrie's study.

They always put poets in Guthrie's study. The old theater man had given Annaghmakerrig to the Arts Councils of both Northern Ireland and the Republic in hopes they would put it to some peaceful use, poised as it is three miles from the border among drumlins and lakes. They put musicians in the refurbished stables, artists and sculptors in the barns. The writers go in the big house—novelists and playwrights upstairs and poets, always and only poets, on the first floor in Tyrone Guthrie's study. It is a large room conducive to larger themes. Even with a bed and armoire, there is plentiful floor space good for pacing. A huge fireplace, high ceilings, and the desk in the lengthy bay windows overlooking the gardens are all suggestive of epic and magnum opus.

What's more, Bernard Loughlin, who only smokes the cigarettes he can borrow or barter for, has found that poets are the most prolific smokers.

Leaning in through the open window that June mid-morning, Bernard tendered in trade, for one of the poet's carefully hand-rolled cigarettes, "a greeny specimen from me humble garden." Robin approved the transaction with a nod, setting the artichoke on the desk.

Robin Robertson gazed out the bay window in search of a theme befitting his surroundings. In black ink centered on the blank page before him he wrote down "Artichoke" and began to work from the memory of the first meal he'd prepared for the woman who would later marry him.

He had steamed them. He'd prepared a side dressing of clarified butter and cilantro.

As they pealed the artichokes they grew contemplative. The table kept them out of reach except for their eyes, which met at intervals then returned to the vegetable duties before them. Their hands grew wet and warm with the pealing. The slow ceremony of food kept them wordless and full of wonder.

The leaves had the texture of secret and private parts, the penetralia of life, where thistle and fuzz and folds give way to pleasure, where touch and taste become the one sensation. He watched her work her tongue and then her teeth and then her lips around the plump, pulpy base of the leaves. And she watched him watching her.

"There now," the woman said, finishing first, the heart exposed. She licked it first, pursing her lips against it, looking at him all the while, and consumed it with the slightest appreciative noise and her eyes closed. He let his fingers work deep into the hairs until the cleanly dampness seemed permanent and the room was filled with the warm aroma of the Mediterranean.

"The rubbed leaves," he wrote, "come away in a tease of green, thinning down to the membrane."

This utterance he divided into four lines, thereby replicating by the pause at each line end, the sacramental pace of the chore the words describe. The reader, he reckoned, should have the facts and the time to savor them.

By mid-summer, the ink on *Nugent v. Nugent* was dry. She got the house and house payments, the car and custody, less of his pension than she had hoped for, and quittance of their marriage bed. He got visitation rights, a schedule of child support payments, most of his dead mother's furniture back, and boxes of his first three volumes of poetry, which had suffered some water damage during the pendency of the matter.

"Deal with it," is what his former spouse told him when he wondered aloud at what had happened to the books. Not mentioned in the court documents, but just as certainly his, were the bitter idioms of pain that began to inform his patois and poetry.

Robin Robertson was preparing clean copy of some poems he was submitting to the poetry editor of *The New Yorker*. The magazine, which bills itself as "possibly the best magazine in the world" is irrefutably among the best possible magazines for poets to publish in. Of the tens of thousands of poems she is sent every year, the editor will publish a hundred or a hundred and twenty. Poets from all over the English-speaking world have tried to nail down what it is, apart from excellence, she responds to in a poem. Her tastes are eclectic, international, utterly unpredictable. But to have a poem in *The New Yorker* guarantees an audience beyond the ordinary pale of poetry. In the best of the "little magazines" and literary quarterlies, a poem's readership is limited to the thousands, or more likely, hundreds of subscribers. But hundreds of thousands across the civilized planet read *The New Yorker*, as they browse in the waiting rooms of stockbrokers, attorneys, gynecologists, and ad agents. It is seen by anthologists, awards committee members, old flames, and perfect strangers. Its shelf life extends to L.A. and London, Hong Kong and Paris, Sydney and Dublin.

Thus, in preparing his manuscript, little wonder Robin Robertson tinkered with revisions of "Artichoke." He changed the last two lines of the first stanza, then changed them back to read "the quick, purpled, beginnings of the male" and replaced the dash after "membrane" with a colon. He wanted, whatever he sent her, to send her excellence.

She took it immediately. She called to thank him for sending it. In due course, a rather generous check came in the mail and page proofs were faxed to his London office.

"Artichoke" appeared in one of the December issues between Henry Nugent's forty-seventh birthday and Christmas Day, both events observed in the company of boxes—books and records not yet unpacked—in the two-bedroom townhouse he had moved into. Whether he or his now distant former wife read "Artichoke" that December cannot be ascertained.

As for Robertson, celebrating the first of several appearances in *The New Yorker*, he retained a reputable child-minder and took his wife out for Lebanese food at Al Hamra in Shepherd Market, where among the menu items are lamb's testicles and, of course, artichoke. They did not, as he told it later, have the balls.

The normal courtesies of copyright prevent my supplying a full text of the poem: fifty-three words in all, deftly distributed between two sextets—twelve lines only, halved by a stanza break. But let me hazard, say, the first three lines of the last stanza so that you might get a feel for the spare language, its flavor. "Then the slow hairs of the heart:" the poet records, "the choke that guards its trophy," and to put a finer point on it he adds, "its vegetable goblet."

If you hold the page at arm's length and squint, it looks like a brief note left on the fridge for a housemate saying what's for dinner, the children are at their grandmother's, don't forget the wine. Or maybe a short list for the market. In a way, it is both. It is an intimate text with plenty of white space and margin. The words are guileless and entirely straightforward in their description of an artichoke being peeled, readied for human consumption.

It is the poem's unfailing penchant for whetting the reader's most private and primary appetites that accounts for its power and, I daresay, its appeal. What is more, this effect upon the reader—the excitement of nerve ends and intentions known only to one's heart of hearts—is uniform, uninhibited by gender or racial or age predictors. You may try this in the comfort of your own home. Try it with friends and passersby. They will blush and grin and ask for a copy.

My friend and mentor, the poet Henry Nugent, went look-ing for the geographic cure. Ohio had become too painful. Seeing the boys hurt his heart. And seeing their mother, whom he stilled loved and mistrusted, was too frequent a reminder of what it was he had lost. "Like going to a wake," he said, "that's never over. The dead need to get buried, eventually." He bought a house. Moved the boxes from the townhouse to the new house, which still didn't feel like home. The boys came over with videos, slept on futons, ate Chicken McNuggets, tried to cope.

He took a sabbatical leave, asked if he could use my cottage in West Clare, flew to Ireland, where he found it, unremark-able for February, cold and damp. The answer, he figured, remarkably, was to drive north: Galway, Sligo, Belfast, the ferry to the lake district, then back in late March to West Clare where I saw him briefly. The weather hadn't much improved.

He seemed terribly agitated. He couldn't sit still. His mis-sion seemed desperate. He was in search of love.

In the months since his marriage ended, he'd had plenty of sex. This is an incumbency known to all of the divorced. Having failed at what is, among other things, a sexual treaty, it is important for men and women alike to demonstrate for any-one who will tolerate it, that It Was Not a Sexual Performance Problem that occasioned the breakup. Thus the comfortable if uninspired sexual patterns of the happily married are replaced by the erotic aerobics of the freshly unwed. New undergar-ments are purchased, sit-ups are done. They bathe more eagerly, clip their nails, invest in creams and lotions and emol-lients. Fresh bed linens, bathrobes, the elements of style and ambience—every encounter is a kind of audition. This is the stuff that memories are made of.

But after a year or so of such encounters, Henry Nugent was hungry for love: that unencumbered approval by another of your species for your presence in their lives.

When he left me in West Clare, he was heading west. He flew back to Ohio, bought a new car with five speeds and bucket seats, drove westward, north, then west again. In April there were postcards from a college town where he'd been booked to do workshops and a poetry reading. Among the people who stood in line after his reading to have him sign their copies of *Good Counsel* was a young poet on the creative writing faculty who touched his arm as she thanked him for his poems, especially the one about a night in a hotel room with his sick son in Cleveland.

May and June brought postcards from Idaho and Montana, Oregon and California. "These hills," he wrote on one, "remind me of Calabria—the sweet foot of Italy—where all beauty is." I didn't know what to make of it.

In July the postcards stopped coming. In mid-August a note came with a snapshot of himself and a striking young woman in a print skirt hugging alongside a river. In the background were mountains. Their bodies had the look of bodies accustomed to one another. The Calabrian references began to make sense.

They had made plans for dinner. The rooms had the well-worn feel of home to him—shelves full of books, tables piled with correspondences and magazines, postcard likenesses of poets and writers, dead but remembered, thumbtacked to the vertical surfaces. Even the kitchen enjoyed the bookish clutter of a woman who cooked to savor rather than to survive and who read over her dinner. Colanders and beakers of olive oil shared cupboard space with review copies of new poetry, her own first volume, and well-worn cookbooks with a regional Italian bias.

And on the refrigerator, held there by kitchen magnets, an aging page out of *The New Yorker* with a poem on it.

"He's my friend's London editor you know."

"Robertson? Really? It's a lovely poem."

Henry considered the penultimate lines of the second stanza: "the meat of it lies, displayed, upended, al dente;".

"It was such a gift in the dead of winter," she said. "When everything is gray and cold and growth seems hopeless."

" 'The stub-root aching in its oil,' " he read aloud.

He had never been so hungry.

"Do you like artichoke?" the woman asked.

In September a card came that said they'd been married. Henry, approaching his birthday this December, calls to say, "It was all your man Robertson's fault, that poem, that 'Artichoke'." Over the phone lines I can feel him grinning.

I tell Robin a version of what the old doctor, William Carlos Williams meant when he wrote that men die everyday for what they miss in poetry. I tell him people are born, and reborn, everyday, who owe their very beings to poems.

Some days I'm sure of God, some days I'm not. Most days I side with the French oddsmaker, Blaise Pascal, whose gambit instructs that it is better to believe in something that isn't than to disbelieve in something that is. And of all God's gifts, the best one is language—the power to name and proclaim and identify, to fashion from the noisy void our lexicons for birds of the air, fishes in the seas, what grows in the greensward; and for contempt and affection, pleasure and pain, beauty and order and their absences. In a world where Someone's in Charge, all of the endings are not happy ones. Nor is every utterance a benediction. But for every death there's some redemption; for every loss an Easter out there with our name on it, for every woe, a return to wooing.

In such a world, my friend and mentor, the poet Henry Nugent, the vocabulary of joy restored to his word horde, writes a poem he entitles "Nines". It is an epithalamium—an ancient form, "upon a bridal chamber"—a wedding poem. "The Song of Solomon" is one—"thou art fair, my beloved, yea, pleasant: also our bed is green." And the ancient Greek Sappho deftly joins references to Hymen, the god of marriage, to those of Ares, the god of war, in her remarkably modern Fragment. There is much coaxing to "raise the ridge-pole higher, higher" because the husband is "taller by far than a tall man" and the builders are exhorted to "pitch the roof-beam, higher, higher" so that your man can "get it through the door."

In his, Henry Nugent enunciates first an understandable caution about the public institution of marriage and, finally, his hope that their "forever" lasts at least thirty years and that the private passions of their wedding night—outside any common law or custom—attend the long nights of their lives together, the math of which he cannot resist calculating in the poem.

There are two stanzas, nine lines each, in loose iambics—the sound of hearts—*daDum, daDum, daDum, daDum, daDum.* Think of Shakespeare: "Did my heart love till now? Forswear it, sight!/For I ne'er saw true beauty till this night."

Perhaps it is this traffic in irony, audibly accomplished, among the numbers and the syllables, where form and function co-conspire toward their common end, that nudges the poetry editor of *The New Yorker* toward the acceptance of Mr. Nugent's poem. She sends him the check and page proofs and her eminent thanks.

My friend and editor, the poet, Robin Robertson, will grin from his office in London. A man well versed in the power of language, he will cut the page from the magazine, take it home and affix it to the refrigerator, where it will move his wife of nine years in ways that are none of our business.

In the fullness of time, however, she will make known her special fondness for the shape and sound of it, the courtesies of copyright do not deter me from sharing here:

Thus we proclaim our fond affirmatives:

I will, I do, Amen, Here Here, Let's
eat, drink and be merry. Marriage is
the public spectacle of private parts:
cheque-books and genitals, housewares, fainthearts,
all doubts becalmed by kissing aunts, a priest's
safe homily, those tinkling glasses
tightening those ties that truly bind
us together forever, dressed to the nines.

Darling, I reckon maybe thirty years,
given our ages and expectancies.
Barring the tragic or untimely, say,
ten thousand mornings, ten thousand evenings,
please God, ten thousand moistened nights like this,
when, mindless of these vows, our opposites,
nonetheless, attract. Thus, love's subtraction:
the timeless from the ordinary times—
nine thousand, nine hundred, ninety-nine.

The Golfatorium

*Write, read, sing, sigh, keep silence, pray,
bear thy crosses manfully; eternal life
is worthy of all these, and greater combats.*

—THOMAS À KEMPIS

It came to me high over California. I was flying across the country to read poems in L.A. I had gigs at the Huntington Library, UCLA, San Bernardino, and Pomona College. And between engagements, four days free to wander at will in Southern California. It was a beautiful blue end of September, the year I quit drinking and my mother died. Crisp and cloudless, from my window seat the nation's geography lay below me. The spacious skies, the fruited plane, the purple mountains' majesty.

I was counting my blessings.

To have such a day for my first transcontinental flight, to have someone else paying for the ticket and the expenses and to be proffering stipends I'd gladly pay taxes on, to say that I was the poet and I had the poems that people in California were paying to hear—these were good gifts. My mother was dying back in Michigan, of cancer. She had told the oncologists, "Enough, enough." They had discontinued the chemotherapy. I was running from the implications.

I was scared to death.

From Detroit we first flew over Lake Michigan then the grainy Midwest and Plains states, then the mountains and valleys of the Great West, and finally the desert west of Vegas and Reno until, in the distance, I could make out the western edges of the San Bernardino Mountains. The Mojave was all dry brown below until, just before the topography began to change from desert to mountain, I saw an irregular rectangle of verdant green. It was the unspeakable green of Co. Kerry or Virgin Gorda purposely transposed to the desert and foothills. I could only hazard a guess at its size—a couple hundred acres I reckoned, though I had no idea what altitude we were flying at. Had we already begun our final descent? The captain had turned on the seat belt sign. All of our seat backs and tray tables were forward.

"Must be a golf course," is what I said to myself. I could see geometrically calculated plantings of trees and irregular winding pathways. "Or a cemetery. Hell!" I remember thinking, "This is California, it could be both!"

In the Midwest we think of California as not just another state and time zone but as another state of mind, another zone entirely, having more in common with the Constellation Orion than with Detroit or Cleveland or Illinois.

And then it came to me, the vision. It *could* be both!

I've been working in secret ever since.

It is no especial genius that leads me to the truth that folks in their right minds don't like funerals. I don't think we need a special election or one of those CNN polls on this. Most folks would rather shop dry goods or foodstuffs than caskets and burial vaults. Given the choice, most would choose root canal work over the funeral home. Even that portion of the executive physical where the doctor says, "This may be a little uncomfortable," beats embalming ninety-nine times out of every hundred in the public races. Random samplings of consumer preference almost never turn up "weeping and mourning" as things we want to do on our vacations. Do you think a funeral director could be elected president? Mine was and is and, godhelpus, ever will be The Dismal Trade. We might be trusted (the last ones to let you down my father used to say) or admired (I don't know how you do it!) or tolerated (well, somebody has to do it) and even loved, though our lovers are often a little suspect (how can you stand to have him touch you after . . . ?). But rare is that man or woman who looks forward to funerals with anything even approaching gladness, save perhaps those infrequent but cheerful obsequies for IRS agents or telemarketers or a former spouse's bumptious attorney.

What's worse, all the advertising in the world won't ever make it an expandable market. Mention of our ample parking, clearance prices on bronze and copper, easy credit terms, readiness to serve twenty-four hours a day does little to quicken in any consumer an appetite for funerals in the way that, say, our taste for fast food can be incited to riot by talk of "two all beef patties, special sauce, lettuce, cheese, pickles, onion on a sesame seed bun." How many of us don't salivate, Pavlovian, when someone hums the tune that says, "You deserve a break today"? A drop in the prime rate will send shoppers out in search of the "big ticket" items—homes, cars, and pleasure craft—but never funerals. Chesty teenagers with good muscle tone dressed in their underwear and come-hither looks can sell us more Chevys than we need, more perfume than we need, more Marlboros than we need, more cruises, more computers, more exercise equipment; more and better, and fewer and better and new and improved and faster and cheaper and sexier and bigger and smaller; but the one funeral per customer rule has held for millennia, and we don't really need a study to show us that for most folks even the one and only is the one too many.

Thus we regard funerals and the ones who direct them with the same grim ambivalence as those who deliver us of hemorrhoids and boils and bowel impactions—*Thanks*, we wince or grin at the offer, *but no thanks!*

There are some exceptions to this quite ponderable truth.

As always, the anomalies prove the rule.

Poets, for example, will almost always regard any opportunity to dress up and hold forth in elegiac style as permissible improvement on their usual solitude. If free drink and a buffet featuring Swedish meatballs are figured in the bargain, so much the better. A reviewer of mine quite rightly calls poets the taxidermists of literature, wanting to freeze things in time, always inventing dead aunts and uncles to eulogize in verse. He is right about this. A good laugh, a good cry, a good bowel movement are all the same fellow to those who otherwise spend their days rummaging in the word horde for something to say, or raiding the warehouses of experience for something worth saying something about. And memorable speech like memorable verse calls out for its inscription into stone. Poets know that funerals and gravesides put them in the neighborhood of the memorable. The ears are cocked for answers to the eternal adverbs, the overwhelming questions. "And may these characters remain," we plead with Yeats, in his permanent phrase, "when all is ruin once again."

And there are elements of the reverend clergy who have come to the enlightenment that, better than baptisms or marriages, funerals press the noses of the faithful against the windows of their faith. Vision and insight are often coincidental with demise. Death is the moment when the chips are down. That moment of truth when the truth that we die makes relevant the claims of our prophets and apostles. Faith is not required to sing in the choir, for bake sales or building drives; to usher or deacon or elder or priest. Faith is for the time of our dying and the time of the dying of the ones we love. Those parsons and pastors who are most successful—those who have learned to "minister"—are those who allow their faithful flocks to grieve like humans while believing like Jews or Christians or Muslims or Buddhists or variants of these compatible themes. They affirm the need to weep and dance, to blaspheme and embrace the tenets of our faiths, to upbraid our gods and to thank them.

Uncles find nickels behind our ears. Magicians pulls rabbits from out of hats. Any good talker can preach pie in the sky or break out the warm fuzzies when the time is right. But only by faith do the dead arise and walk among us or speak to us in our soul's dark nights.

So rabbi and preacher, pooh-bah and high priest do well to understand the deadly pretext of their vocation. But for our mortality there'd be no need for churches, mosques, temples, or synagogues. Those clerics who regard funerals as so much fuss and bother, a waste of time better spent in prayer, a waste of money better spent on stained glass or bell towers, should not wonder for whom the bell tolls. They may have heard the call but they've missed the point. The afterlife begins to make the most sense *after life*—when someone we love is dead on the premises. The *bon vivant* abob in his hot tub needs heaven like another belly button. Faith is for the heartbroken, the embittered, the doubting, and the dead. And funerals are the venues at which such folks gather. Some among the clergy have learned to like it. Thus they present themselves at funerals with a good cheer and an unambiguous sympathy that would seem like duplicity in anyone other than a person of faith. I count among the great blessings of my calling that I have known men and women of such bold faith, such powerful witness, that they stand upright between the dead and the living and say, "Behold I tell you a mystery. . . ."

There are those, too, who are ethnically predisposed in favor of funerals, who recognize among the black drapes and dirges an emotionally potent and spiritually stimulating intersection of the living and the dead. In death and its rituals, they see the leveled playing field so elusive in life. Whether we bury our dead in Wilbert Vaults, leave them in trees to be eaten by birds, burn them or beam them into space; whether choir or cantor, piper or jazz band, casket or coffin or winding sheet, ours is the species that keeps track of our dead and knows that we are always outnumbered by them. Thus immigrant Irish, Jews of the diaspora, Black North Americans, refugees and exiles and prisoners of all persuasions, demonstrate, under the scrutiny of demographers and sociologists, a high tolerance, almost an appetite, for the rites and ceremonies connected to death.

Furthermore, this approval seems predicated on one or more of the following variables: the food, the drink, the music, the shame and guilt, the kisses of aunts and distant cousins, the exultation, the outfits, the heart's hunger for all homecomings.

The other exception to the general abhorrence of funerals is, of course, types of my own stripe whose lives and livelihoods depend on them. What sounds downright oxymoronic to most of the subspecies—a *good* funeral—is, among undertakers, a typical idiom. And though I'll grant some are pulled into the undertaking by big cars and black suits and rumors of riches, the attrition rate is high among those who do not like what they are doing. Unless the novice mortician finds satisfaction in helping others at a time of need, or "serving the living by caring for the dead" as one of our slogans goes, he or she will never stick it. Unless, of course, they make a pile of money early on. But most of us who can afford to send our kids to the orthodontist but not to boarding school, who are tied to our brick and mortar and cash-flow worries, who live with the business phone next to our beds, whose dinners and intimacies are always being interrupted by the needs of others,

would not do so unless there were satisfactions beyond the fee
schedule. Most of the known world could not be paid enough
to embalm a neighbor on Christmas or stand with an old wid-
ower at his wife's open casket or talk with a leukemic mother
about her fears for her children about to be motherless. The
ones who last in this work are the ones who believe what they
do is not only good for the business and the bottom line, but
good, after everything, for the species.

A man that I work with named Wesley Rice once spent all
of one day and all night carefully piecing together the parts of
a girl's cranium. She'd been murdered by a madman with a
baseball bat after he'd abducted and raped her. The morning of
the day it all happened she'd left for school dressed for picture
day—a schoolgirl dressed to the nines, waving at her mother,
ready for the photographer. The picture was never taken. She
was abducted from the bus stop and found a day later in a stand
of trees just off the road a township south of here. After he'd
raped her and strangled her and stabbed her, he beat her head
with a baseball bat, which was found beside the child's body.
The details were reported dispassionately in the local media
along with the speculations as to which of the wounds was the
fatal one—the choking, the knife, or the baseball bat. No
doubt these speculations were the focus of the double post-
mortem the medical examiner performed on her body before
signing the death certificate *Multiple Injuries*. Most embalmers,
faced with what Wesley Rice was faced with after he'd opened
the pouch from the morgue, would have simply said "closed
casket," treated the remains enough to control the odor,
zipped the pouch, and gone home for cocktails. It would have
been easier. The pay was the same. Instead, he started working. Eighteen hours later the girl's mother, who had pleaded to
see her, saw her. She was dead, to be sure, and damaged; but
her face was hers again, not the madman's version. The hair
was hers, not his. The body was hers, not his. Wesley Rice had
not raised her from the dead nor hidden the hard facts, but he

had retrieved her death from the one who had killed her. He had closed her eyes, her mouth. He'd washed her wounds, sutured her lacerations, pieced her beaten skull together, stitched the incisions from the autopsy, cleaned the dirt from under her fingernails, scrubbed the fingerprint ink from her fingertips, washed her hair, dressed her in jeans and a blue turtleneck, and laid her in a casket beside which her mother stood for two days and sobbed as if something had been pulled from her by force. It was the same when her pastor stood with her and told her "God weeps with you." And the same when they buried the body in the ground. It was then and always will be awful, horrible, unappeasably sad. But the outrage, the horror, the heartbreak belonged, not to the murderer or the media or the morgue, each of whom had staked their claims to it. It belonged to the girl and to her mother. Wesley had given them the body back. "Barbaric" is what Jessica Mitford called this "fussing over the dead body." I say the monster with the baseball bat was barbaric. What Wesley Rice did was a kindness. And, to the extent that it is easier to grieve the loss that we see, than the one we imagine or read about in papers or hear of on the evening news, it was what we undertakers call a good funeral.

It served the living by caring for the dead.

But save this handful of the marginalized—poets and preachers, foreigners and undertakers—few people not under a doctor's care and prescribed powerful medications, really "appreciate" funerals. Safe to say that part of the American Experience, no less the British, or the Japanese or Chinese, has been to turn a blind eye to the "good" in "goodbye," the "sane" in "sadness," the "fun" in "funerals."

Thus, the concept of merging the highest and best uses of land, which came to me high over California, seemed an idea whose time had come. The ancient and ongoing duty of the land to receive the dead aligned with the burgeoning craze in the golf business led, by a post-modern devolution, to my vision of a place where one could commemorate their Uncle Larry and work on their short game at the same time—two hundred acres devoted to memories and memorable holes; where tears wept over a missed birdie comingled with those wept over a parent's grave. A *Golfatorium*! It would solve, once and for all, the question of Sundays—what to do before or after or instead of church. The formerly harried husband who always had to promise he'd do the windows "next weekend" in order to get a few holes in during good weather, could now confidently grab his golf shoes and Big Berthas and tell his wife he was going to visit his "family plot." He might let slip some mention of "grief work" or "unfinished business" or "adult-child issues still unresolved." Or say that he was "having dreams" or was feeling "vulnerable." What good wife would keep her mate from such important therapy? What harm if the cure includes a quick nine or eighteen or twenty-seven holes if the weather holds?

So began the dialogue between my selves: the naysayer and the true believer—there's one of each in every one of us. I read my poems in L.A., chatted up the literary set, waxed pithy and beleaguered at the book signings and wine and cheese receptions. But all along I was preoccupied by thoughts of the Golfatorium and my mother dying. When, after the reading at the Huntington Library, I asked the director where would she go if she had four days free in Southern California, she told me "Santa Barbara" and so I went.

There are roughly ten acres in every par four. Eighteen of those and you have a golf course. Add twenty acres for practice greens, club house, pool and patio, and parking and two hundred acres is what you'd need. Now divide the usable acres, the hundred and eighty, by the number of burials per acre—one thousand—subtract the greens, the water hazards, and the sand traps, and you still have room for nearly eight thousand burials on the front nine and the same on the back. Let's say, easy, fifteen thousand adult burials for every eighteen holes. Now add back the cremated ashes scattered in sandtraps, the old marines and swabbies tossed overboard in the water hazards and the Italians entombed in the walls of the club house and it doesn't take a genius to come to the conclusion that there's gold in them there hills!

You can laugh all you want, but do the math. Say it costs you ten thousand an acre and as much again in development costs—you know, to turn some beanfield into Roseland Park Golfatorium or Arbordale or Peachtree. I regard as a good omen the interchangeability of the names for golf courses and burial grounds: Glen Eden and Grand Lawn, like Oakland Hills or Pebble Beach could be either one, so why not both? By and large we're talking landscape here. So two million for property and two million for development, the club house, the greens, the watering system. Four million in up-front costs. Now you install an army of telemarketers-slash-memorial counselors to call people during the middle of dinner and sell them lots at an "introductory price" of, say, five hundred a grave—a bargain by any standard—and *cha-ching* you're talking seven point five million. Add in the pre-arranged cremations at a hundred a piece and another hundred for scattering in the memorial sandtraps and you've doubled your money before anyone has bought a tee time or paid a greens fee or bought golf balls or those overpriced hats and accessories from your pro shop. Nor have you sold off the home lots around the edges to those types that want to live on a fairway in Forest Lawn. Building sights at fifty thousand a pop. Clipping coupons is what you'd be. Rich beyond any imagination. And that's not even figuring how much folks would pay to be buried, say, in the same fairway as John Daly or Arnold Palmer. Or to have Jack Nicklaus try to blast out of your sandtrap. And think of the gimmicks—free burial for a hole in one, select tee times for the pre-need market. And the package deals: a condo on the eighteenth hole, six graves on the par-three on the front nine, dinner reservations every Friday night, tennis lessons for the missus, maybe a video package of you and your best foursome for use at your memorial service, to aid in everyone's remembrance of the way you were, your name and dates on the wall of the nineteenth hole where your golf buddies could get a little liquored up and weepy all in your memory. All for one low price, paid in a way that maximized your frequent-flier miles.

The impulse to consolidate and conglomerate, to pitch the big tent of goods and services is at the heart of many of this century's success stories. No longer the butcher, the baker, the candlestick maker, we go to supermarkets where we can buy meats, breads, motor oils, pay our light bill, rent a video, and do our banking, all in the one stop. Likewise the corner gas station sells tampons and toothpaste (of course, no one comes out to check your oil, nor can the insomniac behind the glass wall fix your brakes or change your wiper blades). Our churches are no longer little chapels in the pines but crystal cathedrals of human services. Under one roof we get day care and crisis intervention, bible study and columbaria. The great TV ministries of the eighties—the Bakkers and Swaggarts and Falwells—were theme parks and universities and hospital complexes that flung the tax-free safety net of God over as much real estate as could be bought. Perhaps the tendency, manifest in many of today's mega-churches, to entertain rather than to inspire, to wow rather than to worship, proceeds from the intelligence, gained generations back, that the big top needed for the tent revival and the three-ring circus was one and the same. Some of these televangelists went to jail, some ran for president, and some rode off into the sunset of oblivion. But they seemed to be selling what the traffic would bear. A kind of one-stop shopping for the soul, where healing, forgiveness, a time-share in the Carolinas, musical ministry, water parks, and pilgrimages to the Holy Land can all be put on one's Visa or Mastercard.

In the same way the Internet is nothing if not an emergent bazaar, a global mall from which one can shop the shelves of a bookstore in Galway, order a pizza or some dim sum, talk dirty to strangers bored with their marriages, and check the demographics of Botswana all without budging from—this would have sounded daft twenty years ago—the "home office."

Thus the paradigm of dual-purpose, high-utility, multitasking applications had taken hold of the market and my imagination.

This had happened to me once before.

Years back before the cremation market really—I can't help this one—heated up, I dreamed a new scheme called "Cremorialization." It was based on the observation that those families who elected to cremate their dead, much as those who buried theirs, felt a need to memorialize them. But unlike earth burial where the memorial took the form of a stone—informative but silent and otherwise useless—those who reduced the dead to ashes and bone fragments seemed to be cheered by the thought that something good might come of something bad, something useful might proceed from what they saw as otherwise useless. Such notions have root in what has been called the Protestant ethic that honors work and utility. The dead, they seemed to be saying, ought to get off their dead ashes and be good for something beyond the simple act of remembrance.

This is the crowd who can always be counted on to say "such a shame" or "what a waste" when they see a room full of flowers at one end of which is a dead human body. The same flowers surrounding a live human body hosting a tea for the visiting professor are, for the most part, "perfectly lovely."

Or when the body amid the gladioli is one recovering from triplets, say, or triple bypass surgery, the flowers are reckoned to be "how very thoughtful." But flowers surrounding a casket and corpse are wasteful and shameful—the money better spent on "a good cause." This notion, combined with cremation, which renders the human corpse easily portable—ten to twelve pounds on average—and easily soluble with new age polymers and resins, brought me to the brainstorm years ago of the dead rising from their ashes, doing their part again—Cremorialization. Rather than dumbly occupying an urn, what old hunter wouldn't prefer his ashes to be used to make duck decoys or clay pigeons? The dead fisherman could become a crank-bait or plastic worms, perhaps given, with appropriate ceremony, to a favorite grandson. The minister's wife, ever the quiet and dignified helpmate, could be resurrected as a new tea service for the parsonage, her name etched tastefully into the saucers. Bowlers could be mixed into see-through bowling balls, or bowling pins, or those bags of rosin they are always tossing. Ballroom dancers could be ocarinas, cat lovers could be memorial kitty litter. The possible applications were endless. The ashes of gamblers could become dice and playing chips, car buffs turned into gear shift knobs or hood ornaments or whole families of them into matching hubcaps. After years spent in the kitchen, what gourmand could resist the chance to become a memorial egg-timer, their ashes slipping through the fulcrum in a metaphor of time. Bookends and knickknacks could be made of the otherwise boring and useless dead. And just as the departed would be made more valuable by becoming something, what they became would be more valuable by placing the word "memorial" in front of it.

We always kept the ashes in a closet—those that weren't picked up by the family or buried or placed in a niche. After ten years I noticed we'd accumulated several dozen unclaimed boxes of ashes. It seemed as if nobody wanted them. I wondered about the limits of liability. What if there were a fire. I tried to imagine the lawsuits—old family members turning up for "damages." There are, of course, damages that can be done even to a box of ashes. We'd call every year around Christmastime to see if the families of these abandoned ashes had come to any decision about what should be done, but more often than not we'd be left holding the box. One Christmas, my younger brother, Eddie, said we should declare it The Closet of Memories and establish a monthly holding fee, say twenty-five dollars, to be assessed retroactively unless the ashes were picked up in thirty days. Letters were sent out. Calls made. Old cousins and step-children came out of the woodwork. Widows long-since remarried returned. The Closet of Memories was near empty by Easter. Eddie called it a miracle.

What I called it was amazing—the ways we relate to a box of ashes—the remains. And all that winter and spring I'd watch as people called to claim their tiny dead, how exactly it was they "handled" it. Some grinned broadly and talked of the weather, taking up the ashes as one would something from the hardware store or baggage claim, tossing it into the trunk of their car like corn flakes or bird seed. Some received the package—a black plastic box or brown cardboard box with a name and dates on it—as one would old porcelain or First Communion, as if one's hands weren't worthy or able or clean enough to touch it. One elderly woman came to claim the ashes of her younger sister. The younger sister's children could not be bothered, though their aunt valiantly made excuses for them. She carried her sister's ashes to the car. Opened the trunk then closed it up again. Opened the back door of her blue sedan then closed that, too. She finally walked around to the front passenger seat, placed the parcel carefully there, paused momentarily, then put the seat belt around it before getting in and driving away. For several it was a wound reopened. And they were clearly perturbed that we should "hassle" them to take some action or else pay a fee. "What do I want with her ashes?" one woman asked, clearly mindless of the possibility that, however little her dead mother's ashes meant to her, they might mean even less to me.

The only mother who mattered was my own. And she was dying of a cancer that reoccurred a year and a half after the surgery that the doctors assured her had "got it all." They had removed a lung. We'd all put away our worst fears and grabbed the ring the surgeons tossed that said "everything was going to be all right." They were wrong. A cough that started at Thanksgiving and was still there at Valentine's Day sent her to the doctor's at my sister Julie's insistence. The doctors saw "an irregularity" in the x-rays and suggested a season of radiation treatments. I supposed this irregularity must be different than the one for which laxatives and diuretics are prescribed. But by June, her body made dry and purple from the radiation, it still had not occurred to me that she would be dying. Even in August, her voice near a whisper, a pain in her shoulder that never left, I clung to the user-friendly, emotionally neutral lexicon of the oncologist, who kept our focus on the progress of the "irregularity" (read tumor) instead of the woman dying before our eyes, whose pain they called "discomfort"; whose moral terror they called "anxiety"; whose body not only stopped being her friend, it had become her enemy.

I never pursued Cremorialization. The bankers and bean counters couldn't be swayed. One said I was probably ahead of my time. He was right. Strange ads turn up in the trade journals now that promise to turn the cremains into objects of art, which bear a uniform resemblance to those marble eggs that were all the rage a few years ago. Oh, once I dumped a fellow's ashes into a clear whiskey bottle that his wife had wired to work as a desk lamp. "He always said I really turned him on," she says and still signs her Christmas cards *Bev and Mel*. Likewise the widow of a man I fished with brought back his ashes after she remarried and asked me to scatter them on the Pere Marquette—the river where we'd fished the salmon run for years. She'd put them in a thermos bottle, one of those big pricey Stanley ones, and said it would be less conspicuous in the canoe than the urn I'd sold her. "Camouflage" she called it and smiled the smile of loss well grieved. But once I got him downstream to one of our favorite holes, I couldn't let him go that way. I buried him, thermos bottle and all, under a birch tree up from the riverbank. I piled stones there and wrote his name and dates on paper, which I put in a fly-box and hid among the stones. I wanted a place that stood still to remember him at in case his son and daughter, hardly more than toddlers when he died, ever took up fishing or came asking about him.

The world is full of odd alliances. Cable companies buy phone companies, softwares buy hardwares. Before you know it we're talking to the TV. Other combinations are no less a stretch: the "motor home," "medicide." By comparison, a cemetery-golf course combo—a Golfatorium—seems, fetched only as far as, you will excuse, a nine iron.

Furthermore, cemeteries have always been widely and mistakenly regarded as land wasted on the dead. A frequent argument one hears in favor of cremation relies on the notion, an outright fiction, that we are running out of land. But no one complains about the proliferation of golf courses. We've had three open in Milford the last year alone. And no one in public office or private conversation has said that folks should take up contract bridge or ping pong or other less land-needy, acreage-intensive pasttimes and dedicate the land, instead, to low-cost housing or co-op organic gardens. No, the development of a golf course is good news to the real estate and construction trades, reason for rejoicing among the hoteliers, restaurateurs, clothiers, and adjoining industries who have found that our species is quite willing to spend money on pleasure when the pleasure is theirs. Land dedicated to the memorialization of the dead is always suspect in a way that land used for the recreation of the living seldom is. There seems to be, in my lifetime, an inverse relationship between the size of the TV screen and the space we allow for the dead in our lives and landscapes. With the pyramids maybe representing one end of the continuum, and the memorial pendant—in which ashes of your late and greatly reduced spouse are kept dangling tastefully from anklet or bracelet or necklace or keychain—representing the other, we seem to give ground grudgingly to the departed. We've flattened the tombstones, shortened the services, opted for more and more cremation to keep from running out of land better used for amusement parks, off-street parking, go-cart tracks, and golf courses. A graveyard gains favor when we combine it with a nature walk or historical tour, as if the nature and history of our mortality were not lesson enough on any given day. We keep looking for community events to have in them— band concerts, birdwatchings—meanwhile, the community events they are supposed to involve, namely funerals and burials, have become more and more private spectacles. It is not enough for it to be only the repository of our dead and the memories we keep of them, or safe harbor for the often noisome and untidy feelings grief includes; comfort and serenity are not enough. We want our parks, our memorial parks, to entertain us a little, to have some use beyond the obvious. Less, we seem to be telling the dead, is more; while for the living, enough is never quite enough.

So the combination of golf and good grieving seems a natural, each divisible by the requirement for large tracts of green grass, a concentration on holes, and the need for someone to carry the bags—caddies or pallbearers.

There will of course be practical arguments—when are you going to actually "do" the burials? Can people play through a graveside service? What is the protocol? Is there a dress code? What about headstones, decoration day, perpetual care? And what, godhelpus, about handicaps? What will the hearse look like? Must we all begin to dress like Gary Player?

When my mother was dying I hated God. Some days when I think of her, dead at sixty-five, I think of how my father said, "These were supposed to be the Golden Years." She bore and birthed and raised nine children because the teachings or the technologies of her generation did not offer reliable "choice." The daughter of a music teacher, she understood everything but "rhythm." It is the strength in numbers I'm the beneficiary of now. The God of my anger was the God she knew—the fellow with the beard and archangels and the abandonment issues. The practical joker with a mean streak, pulling the chair out from under us, squirting us with the boutonniere, shaking our hands with the lightning-bolt joy buzzer and then wondering why we don't "get it"; can't we "take a joke"?

My mother, a Bing Crosby and Ingrid Bergman Catholic, had her heaven furnished with familiar pieces: her own parents, her sister, friends of her youth. Her vision was precise, down to the doilies.

So checking into the Miramar—an old oceanfront hotel south of Santa Barbara, with blue roof tiles over white clapboard, I wanted to hide, for four days only, from the facts of the matter. I remember waking to the sound of pelicans, gulls, and cormorants diving into the blue water, the listless lapping of the waves. The Pacific was pacific. I needed peace. I sat on the deck overlooking the beach. Taut bodies jogged by in primary colors or walked with their designer dogs in the morning light. No one was dying in Santa Barbara. I began to make notes about the golf course-cemetery combo. Would calling it "St. Andrews" be too bold? Would people pay more to be buried on the greens? Would a bad divot be desecration? What about headstones? They'd have to go. But what to replace them with? Memorial balls? These and other questions like them quarreled like children for my attention. I ordered coffee. A grilled cheese sandwich. I avoided the temptation to float in the water. The undulent ocean glistened with metaphor. To sit and watch the sea was good. Everything was going to be all right. By sunset I was transfixed by the beauty. I'd worked out the details of my plan—the location, the capitalization, the ad campaign, the board of directors. Why shouldn't our cemeteries be used for fun and fitness? Pleasure and pain were soluble. Laughing and crying are the same release. I didn't know which I should do next, laugh or weep.

My mother believed in redemptive suffering. The paradigm for this was the crucifixion of Christ, an emblem of which she kept in most rooms of our house. This was the bad day against which all others were measured. She was a student of the fifteenth-century mystic Thomas à Kempis whose *Imitation of Christ* she read daily. "Offer it up for the suffering souls," is what she would say when we'd commence our carping over some lapse in creature comforts. I think it was a Catholic variation on the Protestant work ethic. If you're going to be miserable, her logic held, you may as well be miserable for a good cause.

Who were these suffering souls? I'd ask myself.

Likewise, people of the Irish persuasion have a special knack or affliction for searching out the blessing in every badness. "Happy is the grave the rain falls on," they say as they stand ankle deep in mud, burying their dead, finding the good omen in the bad weather. Thus, in a country where it rains everyday, they have proclaimed the downpour a blessed thing. "Could be worse," they say in the face of disaster or "The devil you know's better than the one you don't," or when all else fails "Just passing through life." Invasion and famine and occupation have taught them these things. They have a mindset that tolerates, perhaps to a fault, God's little jokes on the likes of us.

So when, as a child, I'd find myself hungry or angry or lonely or tired or brutalized by one of the brothers, among my mother's several comforts was the subtle spiritual dictum to "offer it up for the suffering souls." By patient acceptance of pain I could assist in the universal business of salvation. The currency of hurt became the currency of holiness the way you'd change pounds sterling to greenback dollars. God was the celestial bank teller who kept track of the debits and credits to our accounts. Those who died in arrears went to Purgatory—a kind of bump-and-paint shop for the soul, where the dents and dings and rust of life on earth could be fixed before going on to Heaven. Hell was a Purgatory that never ended, reserved for the true deadbeats who not only didn't pay their tolls but didn't figure they owed anyone anything. Purgatory was for rehabilitation. Hell was for punishment, perpetual, eternal, cruel and unusual. The chief instrument of both locales was fire—the cleansing, if painful, flames of purgatorio, the fire and brimstone recompense, for pleasures ill-got and self-indulgent, of the inferno.

I think sometimes that this is why, for most of the last two millennia, the western Church has avoided cremation—because fire was punitive. When you were in trouble with God you went to hell where you burned. Perhaps this created in us feelings about fire that were largely negative. We burned the trash and buried the treasure. This is why, faced with life's first lessons in mortality—the dead kitten or bunny rabbit, or dead bird fallen from its nest on high—good parents search out shoe boxes and shovels instead of kindling wood or barbecues. It is also why we might witness burials, but cremation, like capital punishment, is hidden from us. Of course, Eastern thought has always favored fire as a purifier, as the element that reunites us with our elements and origins. Hence the great public pyres of Calcutta and Bombay, where dead bodies blacken the skies with smoke from their burning.

My mother did not believe this part. Her children needed neither punishment or purification beyond that which she supplied. We were the children of God and her own best efforts. Salvation was a gift of God. Her gift to us was how to claim it. And when, after the Second Vatican Council, they got rid of Limbo and Purgatory, she fashioned it a kind of enlightenment. Still, life had sufferings enough to go around and she wanted us to use them well. It was part of Nature.

"All grievous things are to be endured for eternal life," is how my mother was instructed by Thomas à Kempis. Suffering was thereby imbued with meaning, purpose, value, and reason. Nature passed suffering out in big doses, random and irreverent, but faith and grace made suffering a part of the way by which we make our journey back to God. Atonement meant to be "at one." And this return, this reunion in heaven, this salvation, was the one true reason for our being, according to my mother. This opinion put her, of course, at odds with everything the culture told us about "feeling good about ourselves" or "taking care of numero uno" or the secular trophies of "happiness" and "validation" and "self-esteem." Hers was a voice crying in the suburban wilderness that we were all given crosses to bear—it was our imitation of Christ—and we should offer it up for the suffering souls.

That is how she turned it into prayer—the "irregularity," the cancer, the tumor that moved from her remaining lung up her esophagus, leapt to her spinal cord, and then made for her brain. This was what the doctors said was happening, preferring a discussion of parts failing to persons dying. But for her husband and children what was happening was that her voice was growing more and more quiet, her breath was getting shorter and shorter, her balance was lost to the advance of cancer. My mother was making it work for her, placing the pain and the fear and the grief of it into that account with God she'd kept, by which what was happening to her body became only one of several things that were happening to her. Her body, painful and tumorous, was turning on her and she was dying. I'm sure she was ready to be rid of it. She said her heart was overwhelmed with grief and excitement. Grief at the going from us—her husband of forty-three years, her sons and daughters, grandchildren born and unborn, her sister and brother, her friends. Excitement at the going "home." But as the voice inside her body hushed, her soul's voice seemed to shout out loud, almost to sing. She could see things none of us could see. She refused the morphine and remained lucid and visionary. She spoke words of comfort to each of us—at one point saying we must learn to let go, not only grudgingly, but as an act of praise. I say this not because I understand it but because I witnessed it. I'm not certain that it works—only certain that it worked for her.

Once you've made the leap it's easy. Once you've seen huge tracts of greensward put to seemingly conflicting uses, the world becomes a different place. If golf courses can be graveyards, surely football fields, and soccer pitches, ball diamonds and tennis courts. And what about ski slopes? What folks don't want to be buried on a mountain? Boot Hill we could call it. Listen up, the possible applications are endless. The thrill of victory, the agony of defeat. Life is like that—death is, too.

My mother's funeral was a sadness and a celebration. We wept and laughed, thanked God and cursed God, and asked God to make good on the promises our mother's faith laid claim to in her death. It was Halloween the day we buried her—the eve of All Saints, then All Souls, all suffering souls.

Eddie and I have been looking for acreage. He's a golfer. I'd rather read and write. He says he'll be the Club Pro and I can be the Brains Behind the Operation. We've worked together for years and years. Our sister Brigid does pre-need and our sister Mary has always done the books—payroll and collections and payables. The women seem to control the money. Revenge they call it for our calling it Lynch & Sons.

Whenever I have business at Holy Sepulchre, I stop in section twenty-four, where my mother and father are buried. He lived on after her for two more years. After he was buried we all decided on a tall Celtic cross in Barre granite with their instruction to "Love One Another" cut into the circle that connects the crossed beams. My father had seen crosses like this when I took him to Ireland the year after my mother died. He'd said he liked the look of them.

Stones like these make golf impossible. They stand their ground. It's hard to play through. Those joggers with their designer dogs on leashes and stereos plugged into their ears are not allowed. A sign by the pond reads "No Fishing/Do Not Feed Ducks." The only nature trail in Holy Sepulchre is the one that takes you by the nature of our species to die and to remember.

I miss them so.

I think it's my sisters who plant the impatiens every spring at the base of the stone.

Sometimes I stand among the stones and wonder. Sometimes I laugh, sometimes I weep. Sometimes nothing at all much happens. Life goes on. The dead are everywhere. Eddie says that's par for the course.

Mary & Wilbur

Like all great cities, ours is divided by water. Dublin has its Liffey, London, its Thames. Milford has the Huron River. The Mighty Huron is what knowing locals call it—afloat in the high tide of hyperbole. It is a river that, from its headwaters in Proud Lake, five miles east of town, to the dam at the west end of the village, never works up much of a commotion nor more than one hundred feet of width, except where it fattens in Central Park into what we call the Mill Pond. Of course it flows on westward through Ann Arbor and Ypsilanti and down into Lake Erie, and it begins to look like a real river downstream. You can find it on maps. But here, near its headwaters, it's more of a stream. It is reasonably clean, good for canoers and carp fisherman and raft races. Once a year there's a Duck Race sponsored by the Rotary Club and a good sucker run in early April. Where the train tracks cross over the river at Main Street, there's a trestle they call the Arch and diving from it is against the law—a prohibition largely ignored by local boys for a hundred and fifty years now.

The river divides the south side from the north. It divides the car dealers and liquor stores and light manufacturing shops on the south side from the trendy restaurants, banks, boutiques, and booksellers of the north. The south side has its Southern Baptists, North Main, its Presbyterians. Brakes and mufflers are procured on the south side, diamonds and divorce attorneys on the north.

And as the village is divided by the Mighty Huron so too the souls and psyches of its inhabitants. When it snows we look like Currier and Ives—a Main Street on which neighbors stop to talk, know the merchants they do their business with, nodding and waving their ways between storefronts, grinning for no apparent reason. There's a skating rink in Central Park all winter, and volley ball and tennis in fair weather. And a permanent installation of playground equipment: merry-go-rounds and jungle-gyms. And east and west of Main, old neighborhoods of wooden homes built around the turn of the last century. Each comes with a history well researched by the Historical Society. Five thousand people live in town and ten thousand in the surrounding township. They occupy their cozy homes, shop locally, support their police and volunteer fire departments, and enjoy the usual parades down Main—on Memorial Day and Fourth of July and Christmas. We have Sidewalk Sales and Old Homes Tours, a Classic Car Show and Milford Memories—a festival in August that brings them in from all over the tri-county area. The past three Januarys we've even had an Ice Spectacular—huge blocks of ice brought in and whittled by chainsaws into likenesses of palm trees and dinosaurs. Folks brave the cold to come and see. There is the general sense that the lives we lead here are busy with the neighborly business of making what twenty years from now we intend to call the Good Old Days.

As a past president of the Chamber of Commerce and a Rotarian in good standing, I am delighted to mention our abundant park lands, inland lakes, good schools, and churches, our proximity to hospitals and golf courses, our upmarket home values. And the wide array of services and merchandise locally available at reasonable prices. But as a citizen at large, and the undertaker here, and a witness at the changing of millennia, I'm obliged, as any witness is, to say what happens.

It's a good place to raise families and to bury them.

We've had terrors on both sides of the river. Two girls were found dead here at the end of one summer—stabbed to death and stuffed into a culvert on the wooded west end of Central Park and, in the same park, two years before, a girl kidnapped, raped, and strangled and buried in a shallow grave out in the township by a serial killer who perpetrated similar evils in townships north and south of here. The men who did these wicked things are all in jail and books are being written about them. There is talk of a movie. None of these facts provide a moment's solace. And there have been boys killed by mischief and misadventure. One was found in pieces on the railroad tracks that run behind the west side of Main Street. Whether accident or homicide or suicide has never been determined. Was he walking home, maybe drunk, and was hit by the train, or was he killed and placed there, or did he put himself there and wait for the train to come for reasons we can only imagine? There is still talk of drink, recreational drugs, teen vendettas. As there was when the body of a boy was found hung from the branch of a sugar maple in the woods behind his house. Or when a month after Kurt Cobain, lead singer of Nirvana, blew his head off, one of our local boys came home from school to do the same thing with his father's rifle and Kurt's tune "Rape Me" playing on the tape deck and the fire whistle blaring out across the town.

That whistle is often the first notice we get of damage here—the signal in these parts of disaster. Men drop what they're doing and come on the run—volunteer firemen with lights and sirens rigged to their vans and pickups. They have hoses and oxygen, stretchers and tourniquets. They've been trained in CPR and other heroics. And it is the one shrill note of the fire whistle that proclaims a grass fire or heart attack, car crashes or dead bodies. It is the sound of trouble heard all over the township, of damage or the threat of damage to persons or property. Dogs all over town are driven to howling. Every Saturday at noon they test the thing—a kind of secular Angelus we set our watches by. No one takes much notice on Saturdays. It's only a test. No time to have a heart attack or kitchen fire. The Catholics out on the east end of town have their bells that toll the ancient hours of the daily office. The monkish among us stop and pray. The Presbyterians have restored their carillon that plays, at ten and two and six o'clock, old melodies: "Shall We Gather at the River" and "Abide with Me." So our air is filled with a medley of bells and whistles declaring that in the midst of life, we are in death. God is among us and so is the Devil. The river that runs through this town divides us.

So, while we look, in the right light, like a late-century rendition of the Waltons or Lake Wobegon, there is no shortage here of outrage and heartbreak. There seems to be two topographies—both real but vastly different.

My wife and I take walks at night. She sees the architectural detail of Greek Revival homes, Queen Anne's, Federalist, and Victoriana. I see the garage where two teachers, long married and childless, known for their prowess at ballroom dancing and careful fashions, were found asphyxiated in their Oldsmobile. I remember the perfect penmanship of the note they left explaining their fear of age and infirmity. Or my wife sees a well-made garden, bordering the backyard of a house where I remember painting a bedroom overnight in which a man had shot himself, so that his children, grown now, wouldn't have to return to the mess he'd made. Some things won't cover no matter how many coats we apply. She sees good window treatments, the warm light of habitation where, too often, I see vacancy and absence, the darkness where the light went out. We get along.

And for every home made memorable by death, dozens are made memorable by the lives that were led there utterly unscrutinized by the wider world—lives lived out at a pace quickened only by the ordinary triumphs of daily life: good gladiolas, the well-shoveled walk, the mortgage payments made, the kids through college. Or by the ordinary failures: the bad marriage, the broken water main, trouble with the tax man, the sons and daughters who never call. We know our neighbors and our neighbors' business here. It is the blessing and the curse of the small place. It's getting better lately, and getting worse. As new subdivisions sprout all over the township, we have traffic jams and parking problems, and more privacy. It is a "bedroom" community. Most people work elsewhere. Here is where they come to "get away from it all." People are less curious about one another.

Once there were five bridges over the river. One at Garden Road, at the east end of the township; and one at Mont-Eagle Street—it was also known as Oak Grove Bridge because it provided riverside access to Oak Grove Cemetery. Then one at Huron Street, another at Main, and, finally, one at Peters Road on the west edge of Central Park, just upstream from the dam.

In the early 1970s, the Oak Grove Bridge was declared unsafe for vehicular traffic by the county road commission. Barriers were placed on either side. Bikes and walkers could make it through but cars couldn't. "Bridge Out" is what the signs said. Some months later, the bridge fell into the river, proving, I suppose, beyond all argument, the road commission's point. No one seemed to notice. The only place it went was to the cemetery. There seemed no hurry to repair the bridge. Oak Grove was the elder of two municipal burial grounds in Milford, dating back to the years before the Civil War, when farmers and mill workers first made a town here. Oak Grove had served the township well, taking the dead for a hundred and fifty years—old families our roads are named after, rooted to places, settled in, in ways the highly mobile types of the late twentieth century do not comprehend. Where our ancestors stayed, we move, twenty percent of us every year, from east coast to west coast, from starter home to dream house, from condos to time shares and retirement villages. The dead and buried remain, for the most part, immobile, eating the dust of new aging generations who have learned to travel light and fast and frequently and put some distance between themselves and their dead. One of the obvious attractions of cremation is that it renders our dead somehow more portable, less "stuck in their ways," more like us, you know, scattered.

But just as Dante had his Lethe and Venice has its Zattere, the slow corteges that crossed the Huron over Oak Grove Bridge, all those years ago, no doubt took note of the evident metaphor—that the dead parent or child or sibling had gone to another shore, another side, changed utterly into townspeople of another dimension.

When the kids were little, we fished off the bridge abutments on summer evenings and watched the bats fly out from the trees in Oak Grove to feast in the buggy air over the river. Sometimes I'd take them there to get rubbings of headstones to match new granite to old designs as elder stragglers of the old families were buried, shipped back home oftentimes from Florida or Arizona or North Carolina. We'd walk among the old trees and monuments trying to imagine the lives they marked. They would ask me questions about the way things worked. It was where I learned the answer "I don't know." What I did know was that Oak Grove was different from the newer cemeteries, where people hustled back to their cars and back to their lives the minute the minister was done with the benediction. At Oak Grove people would remain, trading news of graduations, marriages, grandchildren. They would browse among the neighboring stones of long dead elders with the look on their faces you see in libraries and museums where we study the lives and work of others to learn about ourselves. And the stones had a presence, huge by today's standards. They could not be walked over or mowed over. Likewise, they told, in the eloquent plain chant of the stonecutter, not only the facts but some of the features. Kin was buried with kin. Lots were bought eight graves at a time, or ten. Folks stayed put. Nor has Oak Grove any "chapel" for indoor services—that tidy enterprise whereby the dead are left unburied while the family goes back to their lives, untroubled by inclement weather or harsh realities. A burial at Oak Grove means dirt, a hole in the ground, contending with the "elements."

Among the several duties of a funeral is, of course, the disposal of the dead for the living's sake. And this trip—taken for long years from the corner of Liberty and First Streets, where our funeral home has always been, down Atlantic Street to Mont-Eagle Street, and over the bridge—passed in its three-quarter-mile route, not factories or shops or shopping malls, but homes—brick and clapboard, large and small, but homes. The dead were put, properly, out of our homes but not out of our hearts, out of sight but not out of town.

Thus, Oak Grove always seemed a safe extension, a tiny banishment of the dead from the living, a kindly stone's throw away—a neighborhood of its own, among whose stones the living often spent their Sunday afternoons picnicking among the granite suburbs of grandparents, spinster aunts, ne'er-do-well uncles kept alive in the ordinary talk of the living. Geraniums were planted for "Decoration Day," flags stuck in the graves of old soldiers, grass clipped around headstones all summer, leaves raked and mums planted in the fall, and grave blankets placed before the first snows of winter. The distance between the dead and the living seemed no greater than the river. Neither strange nor embarrassing, the dead were only dead, no less brothers and sisters, parents, children, friends. And death was considered part of the nature of things in a culture where crops failed, cattle starved, and neighbors died. They were waked, eulogized, buried, and grieved. And against forgetfulness, huge stones were hauled in with names and dates on them to proclaim their permanent place in our townscapes. It is this ancient agreement—the remembrance of the dead by the living—that accounts for all burial grounds and most statuary and entire histories.

After Oak Grove Bridge fell into the Mighty Huron, we took a longer, more complicated route through town: First to Commerce, then westbound to Main, then south through the middle of the town with its gridlock and onlookers, and over the Main Street Bridge to Oakland Street on the south side. Left on Oakland past the abandoned jelly factory, the long-filled city dump, across the railroad tracks, and into the back entrance of Oak Grove. It wasn't much of an inconvenience except for the terrible repair of Oakland Street, which had badly decomposed from years of inattention. There were pot holes in it small cars could be lost in, and we'd always have to wash our fleet—the hearse and flower car and family car, covered invariably in dust or mud or slush. And there was some difference, though I never heard it said, between crossing the river and crossing the railroad tracks, between marsh banks full of waterfowl and the town dump with old Impalas rotting on their rims, between the backyards bordered with perennials and the factory yard surrounded by chain-link and barbed wire.

Still, no one regarded it as much of a hardship—this rerouting of funerals from a primarily domestic route to a primarily commercial one. And, washing the hearse afterward I'd content myself that it was somehow good for business to take our shiny black parades through town, all flags and flashers and police escorts, letting the locals get a look at how well we directed funerals.

Except for a fellow who wrote a really fine auto parts manual, I was the only published writer alive in town for several years. Then a local Vietnam veteran wrote and published his memoir of that war and there were three of us literary stars in Milford's firmament. But I was the only poet. And like most poets who want to live amiably among their neighbors, I had avoided any temptation to read them my poems. For their part, my townspeople, like the population at large, were pleased to have a poet living among them, in the way we approve of good infrastructure and school systems, so long as we don't have to pay too close of attention. And a poet in the environs is handy if you need a poem for a special occasion—the in-laws' anniversary or the retirement of clergy, or the matriculation of high school students every June. I drew the line on such activities years back when the owner of the local Dairy Queen asked me for something to commemorate the opening of a satellite location by the entrance to the metropark. "No" is what I told him and was resolved to tell any others evermore. No amount of coaxing could change my mind.

Then Mary Jackson called.

Mary lives in Milford half of each year in the house on Canal Street, two blocks from the funeral home, that her parents and her grandparents lived in. The other half of every year she lives and works in Hollywood in the movies and TV and theater. Maybe her most memorable part was of Miss Emily, one of the spinsterly Baldwin sisters on "The Waltons," which was popular in the seventies and early eighties and still can be seen in reruns on cable. Mary was the tiny smiling sister who would spike the punch at Christmastime with their father's recipe and make John-Boy and Susan and Grandpa and Gramma all a little tipsy in a way we approved of in horse-and-buggy days.

When Mary isn't acting or living in Hollywood, she comes home to Milford as she has for years. Friends visit from New York and London and L.A.—theater types of all ages and persuasions who probably think of themselves as "on location" here. It makes Mary seem ageless, which, of course, she is. She takes them to dinner uptown and introduces them to friends and neighbors over teas in her parlor.

All of Mary's people are buried in Oak Grove. There's a bench made of Barre granite, hand cut in Vermont, with JACKSON on it. And a stone with Mary's own name on it—her married name actually, "Mary Jackson Bancroft"—the details of the marriage and its end, unknown to us. But Mary has staked her claim in Oak Grove and has every intention of being buried there.

When word first got to Mary about the collapse of the bridge, she was disturbed. When it became clear that no plan for its repair was in the works, she was quietly outraged. The Village and the Township offices proffered "money problems" in answer to her first inquiries. The county road commission could not promise action. Its budget had been pushed to the limits by boom times in the county. As country roads became major thoroughfares, old farms turned into subdivisions, how could they spend money "on the dead" when the living needed to get to school and to work and to church and to the shopping mall? How, they argued, convincingly, could a case be made for the dead's convenience, when the living lived with such inconvenience?

Mary came to see me. She said she wanted to make her "arrangements." She brought a list a pallbearers and alternates—stunt doubles she called them. She said I should read a poem—"The Harp-Weaver" by Edna St. Vincent Millay—and that the Methodist minister should do the rest. That she trusted me with the ultimate theater I took as high praise. She said it was a shame about Oak Grove. "The bridge, you know. Something should be done." Then she told me she had made a decision. She steadfastly refused to be buried by way of the back door of Oak Grove. In all of her eighty plus years, she explained, she had seen, in her mind's eye, the tasteful little procession leaving the funeral home by First Street, detouring slightly down Canal and right on Houghton, thus passing her house (the hearse pausing briefly according to custom), then left on Atlantic, right at Mont-Eagle, then down to the river, crossing by the bridge under the high gate of Oak Grove to rest in the companionable earth there. She would not, she insisted, be a "spectacle," processing down through town while strangers shopped in the dime store or browsed in the sale racks of Arms Brothers or Dancers Fashions.

I am not ashamed to say that for a funeral director, the refusal of one of a town's most cherished and well-heeled citizens to be buried in the ground intended for her, is a threat to be taken seriously. It's the kind of thing that could catch on. I tendered other options for crossing the river. Perhaps a barge, Viking style, with the mourners ferried back and forth, à la Dante? "Like Elvis on that ridiculous raft?" she said. "Floating around those man made lagoons in Blue Hawaii?—Never! Not even over may dead body!"

We could drive a little east, I lamely suggested. The Garden Road bridge was still intact, wonderfully remote—"far from the maddening crowd," I said—but Mary would not hear of it. No detours, no barges, no catapults, no excuses. She was going the way she intended to go, the way her mother and father and her uncles and brothers had gone, over the Oak Grove Cemetery Bridge. It would have to be repaired.

Truth told, Mary Jackson had the wherewithal, no doubt, to write a check and have a new bridge done—still working in her eighties and the royalties still coming in has its rewards. But being a good American, she formed a committee, knowing that the problem was not only one of finance but of perception. She called Wilbur Johnson, her neighbor and old friend. His own darling Milver had suffered the indignity of the Main Street route just months before. Wilbur agreed something had to be done.

Wilbur Johnson knew everyone in town. It was his style. For seventy years he'd worked in the produce section of the local market, proffering welcome to newcomers and old timers over heads of lettuce and ears of sweet corn. The market first owned by his father and then by his brother had changed hands a couple more times since Wilbur's youth. But Wilbur always went with the deal—an emblem of those times when people came away from the market with more than what they'd bought. Once known by Wilbur, you were known. Unafraid of growth and change, he thrived on the lives of those around him from children in shopping carts, their young mothers, husbands sent to market with a list, bag boys, and cashiers. His own life, perfectly settled—he never changed jobs or wives or churches or houses—gave him an appetite for changes in the lives of others. He kept an open ear for the names of newborns and newlyweds, news of setbacks and convalescences, the woeful monologues of the jilted, the divorced, the bereaved. He remembered the names of children, visiting in-laws, friends of friends. He had a good word for everyone and everyone knew him. Nowadays we call this "networking" and the store of information Wilbur kept on the lives of others, a "data base." But Wilbur called it "neighborly"—the attention we pay to each other and each other's lives.

Mary and Wilbur became the co-chairs of the committee. They called some of the other old timers in town—descendants of the Ruggles brothers who founded the town in the early nineteenth century, Armstrongs and Arms, Wilsons and Smiths. Meetings were scheduled, mission statements made, pictures taken. Articles began to appear in *The Milford Times*. An account was opened in the bank. Appeals for matching funds were faxed to county commissioners and state representatives and senators whose staffs sent back well-worded letters full of good wishes and intent that, all the same, managed to thread the needle between a certain Yes or No. They wanted to make it perfectly clear, though what "it" was remained a mystery.

The effort, in the minds of most of us, was noble but doomed to failure. Teenagers and young marrieds never thought about cemeteries, being immortal. Folks in their thirties, busy with starter homes and credit-card debt could not be counted on for cash. And the baby boomers in their forties planned to be buried in Milford Memorial—a sumptuous and well-kept memorial park with flat markers and easy maintenance—the commemorative equivalent to the lackluster subdivisions that sprouted in the fifties where every house looked like the next and the lawns were well maintained in a purgatory of sameness. Or they planned to be cremated and scattered in some far-off and really meaningful locale—a favorite fishing hole or golf course or shopping mall. Or they simply did not think of it at all, trying to keep, in the parlance of the generation, "their options open." Among fifty-year-olds, trying to maintain the fiction that they were still in "middle age" and would all, accordingly, live to be a hundred, the mention of cemeteries was strictly taboo, conflicting as it did with those old lies about life beginning at fifty and it being such "a great time to be silver!" A bridge to reconnect us to an old cemetery, rarely used for new burials, occupied the nethermost place on the totem-pole of worthy causes. Public and private beneficence seemed better spent on the homeless, the addicted, the battered and disenfranchised; the living not the dead.

So when Mary called to ask me to compose a poem to be read at the dedication ceremonies she saw in the future, I told her, "Yes, yes of course, I'd be honored etc. . . . ," breaking my long-standing ban on occasional poems with the thought in mind that she would never get it done. The bridge, the poem, the whole project would lapse, in time, into the rosy realms of well-intentioned but never realized dreams. The good old days, like the lives of Miss Emily Baldwin and John-Boy Walton, of Mary and Wilbur and the rest of the sepia-colored characters that populate the home towns of our memories, were gone. Gone forever. No money would be spent on metaphor while real needs were so great.

All the same, Wilbur kept talking and Mary kept lobbying and those of us who loved them hadn't the nerve to prepare them for the eventual disappointment. "Keep up the good work," is what we'd say when we saw them. "Something good will surely come of it." To be sure, Mary and Wilbur began to look like ambassadors, emissaries of a time long gone when folks took seriously their connections to the dead, their access to them, their memories. Memories, after all, were what they were peddling—good old days, or so it seemed—when the dead were somehow different from the dead today.

Of course, those days, like the ones we occupy, had no shortage of heartache in them. At the turn of the last century, more than half the deaths recorded were the deaths of children under twelve. The life expectancy was forty-seven years. Men marched off to war and died. Women died in childbirth. Everyone was born with a dose of mortality. In this way they were terribly modern. And the parents of children dead nowadays of AIDS bear more than passing resemblance to the parents of cholera victims a few generations back, or small pox or the flu. And the widowed then, like the widowed now, trade passion for remembrance of passion. But somehow, memories of the dead seemed more accessible, the dead themselves not so estranged.

I often think about this schizophrenia, how we are drawn to the dead and yet abhor them, how grief places them on pedestals and buries them in graves or burns the evidence, how we love and hate them all at once; how the same dead man is both saint and sonovabitch, how "the dead" are frightening but our dead are dear. I think funerals and graveyards seek to mend these fences and bridge these gaps between our fears and fond feelings, between the sickness and the sadness it variously awakens in us, between the weeping and dancing we are driven to at the news of someone's dying. The man who said that all deaths diminish me was talking about the knowledge at the edges of every obit that it was not me and someday will be.

Thus, graveyards are a way of keeping the dead handy but removed, dear but a little distant, gone but not forgotten.

No doubt the impulse to do this—to get the dead to their own quarters was, at first, olfactory. The Neanderthal widow, waking to the dead lump of her man likely figured he was only being quiet or lazy. Was it something he'd eaten? Something she'd said? It might have been hours before she knew something was different. Here was a preoccupation or an indifference she'd never seen before. But not until his flesh started rotting did the idea come to her to bury him because he'd been changed utterly and irretrievably and, if her nose could be trusted, not for the better. Thus the grave is first and foremost a riddance. But this other impulse—to memorialize, to commemorate, to record has a more subtle motive. I think of Bishop Berkeley's tree, requiring someone to hear it fall. We need our witnesses and archivists to say we lived, we died, we made this difference. Where death means nothing, life is meaningless. It's a grave arithmatic. The cairns and stone piles, the life stories drawn on cave walls, the monuments in graveyards, one and all, are the traces left of the species before us— a space that they've staked out in granite and bronze. And whether a pyramid or Taj Mahal, a great vault in Highgate or a name on The Wall, we let them stand. We visit them. We trace the shapes of their names and dates with our fingers. We say the little epitaphs out loud. "Together forever." "Gone but not forgotten." We try to reassemble their lives from the stingy details, and the exercise teaches us something about how to live.

Is it kindness or wisdom, honor or self-interest?

We remember because we want to be remembered.

Mary Jackson can bring the dead to life. In reminiscences launched over luncheons or teas or walks through Oak Grove, she restores them to us. In her narratives, the dead become perfectly modern, given to the same fits of joy and sorrow as

ourselves. As when her Uncle Nick Stephens, in Mary's childhood, came across a stone on the Crawford lot that read:
"Behold me now as you pass by. As you are now, so once was
I. As I am now soon you will be. Prepare for death and follow
me." A good Victorian epitaph, memorable and morbid, a jin-
gle in the stonemason's best script. To which Uncle Nick,
never at a loss for words, replied on the spot: "To follow you
I won't consent until I know which way you went."

We buried Wilbur Johnson a few years back. He was put in
the grave at Oak Grove next to Milver and his name and dates
carved into the stone. I see him striding up the steps of my
office twenty-five years ago to ask if I was the new funeral
director in town. "Well you're a man I'll need to know," is
what he said and then he said I could pick him up on the following Wednesday and drive him to the Chamber of
Commerce luncheon. Wilbur always went more than half way
when it came to welcomes. And I can see him, in his last year,
arm in arm with Mary Jackson in the ceremonial crossing of
Oak Grove Bridge, the new bridge built by their determination, to cut the ribbon and open it to the general public. Bands
were assembled, politicos, old soldiers from the VFW, the reverend clergy. It was a bright blue morning at the end of May—
Memorial Day. Townspeople gathered at the river to watch the
festivities. A microphone had been rigged up with loudspeak-
ers in the trees. Wilbur thanked all of the committee for their
tireless efforts. The Village President said wasn't it a fine thing.
The state senator was pleased to have helped with a grant from
the Department of Commerce and read off the names of people in Lansing. Then Mary read the poem I'd written when it
began to look like she'd actually get it built. And people stood
among the stones and listened while Mary's voice rose up over
the river and mingled in the air with the echo of Catholic bells
tolling and tunes in the Presbyterian steeple and the breeze with
the first inkling of June in it working in the fresh buds of winter oaks. The fire whistle was silent. No dogs howled.

Mary has the gift of voices. When she speaks the words, she sounds like one of our own. And the words, when she says them, sound like hers and hers alone.

"At the Opening of Oak Grove Cemetery Bridge"

Before this bridge we took the long way around
up First Street to Commerce, then left at Main,
taking our black processions down through town
among storefronts declaring *Dollar Days!*
Going Out of Business! Final Mark Downs!
Then pausing for the light at Liberty,
we'd make for the Southside by the Main Street bridge
past used car sales and party stores as if
the dead required one last shopping spree
to finish their unfinished business.
Then eastbound on Oakland by the jelly-works,
the landfill site and unmarked railroad tracks—
by bump and grinding motorcade we'd come
to bury our dead by the river at Oak Grove.

And it is not so much that shoppers gawked
or merchants carried on irreverently.
As many bowed their heads or paused or crossed
themselves against their own mortalities.
It's that bereavement is a cottage industry,
a private enterprise that takes in trade
long years of loving for long years of grief.
The heart cuts bargains in a marketplace
that opens after-hours when the stores are dark
and Christmases and Sundays when the hard
currencies of void and absences
nickel and dime us into nights awake
with soured appetites and shaken faith
and a numb hush fallen on the premises.

Such stillness leaves us moving room by room
rummaging through cupboards and the closetspace
for any remembrance of our dead lovers,
numbering our losses by the noise they made
at home—in basements tinkering with tools
or in steamy bathrooms where they sang in the shower,
in kitchens where they labored over stoves
or gossiped over coffee with the nextdoor neighbor,
in bedrooms where they made their tender moves;
whenever we miss that division of labor
whereby he washed, she dried; she dreams, he snores;
he does the storm window, she does floors;
she nods in the rocker, he dozes on the couch;
he hammers a thumbnail, she says Ouch!

This bridge allows a residential route.
So now we take our dead by tidy homes
with fresh bedlinens hung in the backyards
and lanky boys in driveways shooting hoops
and gardens to turn and lawns for mowing
and young girls sunning in their bright new bodies.
First to Atlantic and down Mont-Eagle
to the marshy north bank of the Huron
where blue heron nest, rock-bass and bluegill
bed in the shallows and life goes on.
And on the other side, the granite rows
of Johnsons, Jacksons, Ruggles, Wilsons, Smiths—
the common names we have in common with
this place, this river and these winteroaks.

And have, likewise in common, our own ends
that bristle in us when we cross this bridge—
the cancer or the cardiac arrest
or lapse of caution that will do us in.
Among these stones we find the binding thread:

old wars, old famines, whole families killed by flues,
a century and then some of our dead
this bridge restores our easy access to.
A river is a decent distance kept.
A graveyard is an old agreement made
between the living and the living who have died
that says we keep their names and dates alive.
This bridge connects our daily lives to them
and makes them, once our neighbors, neighbors once again.

Sweeney

~

Sweeney: Ah! Now the gallows trap has opened
that drops the strongest to the ground!
Lynchseachan: Sweeney, now you are in my hands,
I can heal these father's wounds:
your family has fed no grave,
all your people are alive.

SEAMUS HEANEY, *SWEENEY ASTRAY*

My friend, the poet, Matthew Sweeney, is certain he is dying. This is a conviction he has held, without remission, since 1952 when he first saw the light, in its gray Irish version, in Ballyliffin, in northernmost Donegal. He knew even then, though he was some years from the articulation of this intelligence, that something was very, very wrong.

What was it the pink infant Sweeney sensed, aswaddle in his bassinet, warmed by the gleeful cooing of his parents, a peacetime citizen of a green and peaceful place, that made him conscious of impending doom?

Nor did his more or less idyllic childhood, his education at the Malin National School, his successful matriculation from the Franciscans at Gormanstown, nor his successful escape from university—first from Dublin, then from North London Polytechnic, and finally from Freiburg University (where he befriended, for reasons soon to be illumined, a corps of medical students)—or any of the several other blessing this life bestows, disabuse him of the sense, continuously a part of his psychology, that there was a deadly moment in every minute; an end with his name on it ever at hand.

Even after his successful wooing of the most beautiful woman in the neighboring parish, the former Rosemary Barber of Buncrana, praised in local song and story for the fierceness of her eyes, the depth of her intellection, the lithe perfection of her form, and the sensibilities of character—even after such a triumph the niggling gloom that attended his conviction, far from going hush, grew louder still. For now he had not only a life to lose but a life made precious by the blissful consortium of married life. (A consortium on which his forthcoming collection *The Bridal Suite* will no doubt shed inspired light.) In like manner, the birth of his daughter Nico, his heart's needle if ever was, followed by the birth of his son Malvin, who soon enough would call him *Daddy*, made him immediately happier and accordingly sadder.

If you love your life in this world, Matthew remembered Paul opining, *you will lose it*. He loved his life. What sane man wouldn't. Loss, he figured, stalked him with its scythe.

He'd written poems. He liked the sound of words of his own making in his own mouth. He'd met with early and deserved critical success. The Sweeneys had long since settled in London, the better to pursue his literary career. The better, likewise, for a man whose fear of driving was, by his own admission, consummate—a dread driven by visions of his body and the bodies of his children entangled with metal to their disadvantage. London, with its Underground, buses, and reliable taxi hacks, unlike the hinterlands of Donegal, gave Matthew the mobility he needed without the morbidity risked by driving a car. What's more, the Kingdom's capital is one of the great ambulatories of the world, providing access, at every turn, to the retail purveyors of essential and elective goods.

Thus, from the stoop of his ample flat in Dombey Street, Matthew Sweeney need only travel eastward less than two hundred meters whereupon he finds himself in Lambs Conduit Street—a walking mall of small shops and markets. Within a stone's throw of his premises is a pharmacist (to whom Mr. Sweeney addresses frequent queries), a French bakery for croissants, a florist (from whom Mr. Sweeney purchased the wee cacti that became the title poem of his most recent and acclaimed collection), his local public house, The Lamb (for the usual wetgoods), a dry cleaners, two coffee shops, a grocery and a greengrocer (with whom Mr. Sweeney has long debated the use and abuses of diverse lettuces, aubergine, and chili peppers), two victualers (one Irish, one Prussian), an herbalist (on whose custom I am unqualified to comment), and the Bloomsbury office of A. France Undertakers—one of London's eldest and most respected carriage-trade mortuaries, passing by whose black and gilded storefront, Mr. Sweeney can be observed to quicken his pace and heard to whistle the fragments of a Tom Waits tune. Only the loss, in 1991, of Bernard Stone's Turret Bookshop (which housed the city's most comprehensive selection of contemporary poetry along with Bernard Stone himself) diminished the hospitable cityscape outside the Sweeneys' door.

One block due north of which, it is worthy of notice, stands the ancient and imposing structure of The Royal London Homeopathic Hospital. No one of the hundreds of poets and writers who have made their pilgrimage to Matthew's home regards this proximity as happenstance. But whether the availability of emergency care or the endless parade of distressed humanity within eyeshot of his fourth-floor living room adds to or subtracts from Matthew's angst is anyone's guess. Maybe Sweeney himself doesn't know. But his frequent foot travels west into Queen's Square to meet with his man at Faber & Faber, the publisher of Matthew's children's poems (whose appeal, according to reviewers, proceeds from their dark homage to monsters and menace and the inherent dangers of maturation), take him, inevitably, by the hospital's massive edifice.

Indeed, the Sweeney home in Bloomsbury (a place name from which a wordsmith of Matthew's caliber can easily extract the vital and the morbid etymological strains) sits at an epicenter of the medical forces, to wit: the Royal College of Surgeons, the London University Hospital, the Society of Endocrinologists, Her Majesty's Hospital for Neurological Disease, the Hospital for Tropical Diseases (where Matthew once left samples of urine and sputum to be screened for the Ebola virus), which, along with other regiments of the medical militia, all within walking distance, speak to the battle being endlessly waged between man (in the gender inclusive sense) and the microbial forces of nature by which he (see above) is infested, infected, afflicted, endangered, diseased, and ulti-mately—and this is Matthew's point—put to death.

Perhaps a little history here. It was in Bewley's Museum over Grafton Street where I first met Matthew Sweeney. It was Dublin and springtime of 1989. The Irish launch of his fourth collection, *Blue Shoes*, occurred but the day before a reading I was giving in the upper room of the famous coffee emporium. He prevailed upon his editor, now our editor, to stay in Dublin an extra day so the two of them might come to my reading. One of our Dublin friends in common, Philip Casey, the poet and novelist, had given me Matthew's poems and given Matthew some of mine. There followed a genial corre-spondence on themes of admiration and shared acquaintance that prefaced our meeting face to face. We repaired to Grogan's Bar according to the local custom. I was touched by his generous praise for my reading, by his interest in my occupational familiarity with the grisly dimensions of disease and pathology, and by his apparent preference for black attire, a preference I share of practical necessity.

The audience was too brief, the barroom too noisy, I was jet-lagged, and Matthew, not fully recovered from the night before. Happily, it was the first of many meetings since, in England and in Ireland and in Michigan, where each of us has enjoyed the comforts of the other's home, the company of the other's wife, the wonderments of the other's children, and the society of the other's friends. To which abundance must be added the dialogue of each other's poems, in which reviewers have found different treatment of similar themes—of domestic perils, imminent damage, and the transcendent properties of death.

Among the society of writers and foodies (about which, more anon) he keeps in London, Matthew is fashioned a charming neurotic of the hypochondriacal variety. There are accounts of his inflation of the common cold to pneumonia or tuberculosis. His headaches are all brain tumors; his fevers, meningitis; his hangovers, all peptic ulcers or diverticulitis. Any deviations from the schedule of his toilet are bowel obstructions or colon cancer. He has been tested for every known irregularity except pregnancy, though he takes, on a seasonal basis, medication for PMS from which, no one doubts, he suffers. He is a consumer of medical opinion and keeps a list of specialists and their beeper numbers on his person. A cardiologist, an acupuncturist, an immunologist, an oral surgeon, an oncologist, a proctologist, and a behavioral psychologist join several psychic and holistic healers from regional and para-religious persuasions to make up Matthew's medical retinue. The same numbers are programmed on speed-dial from his home phone. And where most of his co-religionists wear a medallion that reads *In Case of Emergency Call a Priest*,

Sweeney's reads *Call an Ambulance. Call a Doctor. Please Observe Universal Precautions.*

He has consulted for or imagined having every known malady of the human species from Albers-Schönberg disease to Zygomycosis infection and seems strangely uplifted by the transmigration of ailments between genus and sub-groups heretofore unknown. Thus, swine flu, deer tick disease, feline leukemia, brown bat rabies, and, of course, parrot fever must be ruled out at his quarterly physical exams.

He is, and will suffer no quarrel on this account, the only known survivor of mad cow disease, caught, he insists, from the meagre-most portion of tenderloin that accompanied kippers and poached eggs at Simpsons-on-the-Strand, where he brunched, by appointment, with the restaurant reviewer for the London *Observer*. Their discussion of mushrooms in Southern French cuisine apparently filled Matthew with such overwhelming images of toxicity that the paramedics had to be called.

The standing joke is that Matthew possesses an open offer of a sizable advance from a prominent publisher for an intimate treatise on hypochondria, which, alas, he has never felt well enough to do.

But while others nod and wink and roll their eyes, I have come to wonder if he isn't a harbinger, a kind of visionary, a prophet, a voice crying out in the urban desert, *The End Is Near, It's Later than You Think.*

It was not only the commuter services or the literary milieu or the world-class health care that brought Sweeney to London. It was the food. Unimaginative about the preparation of food, the British have brought the best from the far reaches of the former Empire to London. There is no regional or national or ethnic cuisine on the face of the planet that does not have an office in London. And Matthew has made it his mission to sample and to savor and to study each. He is a student of the palate and the plate, a sage of the taste buds, tongue, and tablefare. In this incarnation he has found the best Thai eatery (Tui in South Kensington, near the offices of Secker & Warburg), the best Afghan (The Caravan Serai in Paddington Street), the best Indian (The Red Fort in Soho), the finest dim-sum (Harbor City in Chinatown), the ultimate noodle-bar (Wagamama in Streathern Street behind the British Museum), the most reliable vegetarian curry (Mandeer in an alleyway behind Tottenham Court Road Station). The geography of taste is as boundless for a man as the sky is borderless to flighted birds. And Sweeney often seems—rapt in sampling some hitherto unknown morsel—almost winged with delight, a rare bird of an urban paradise.

But where the goldfinch craves thistle and the pelican, fish, and the hummingbird, nectar, and the peregrine, meat; the free-range of Matthew's hankerings is suited to the city's cosmopolitan menu and he plots his daily flights according to a constellation of favorites that shine brightly in his firmament of food. On these crusades he is often accompanied by willing accomplices from the arts of verse or gourmandery for whom a meal shared with Matthew Sweeney is a tuition they are more than happy to pay. (Here, as elsewhere, the temptation to drop names, well known in the world of letters and epicures, is nearly unavoidable. But I was better raised than that. To err by silence is better than omission.)

I should also say he is a superior cook who takes seriously every aspect of the selection, the preparation, the presentation, and the savoring of whatever bears the insignia of his kitchen.

All of which I mention because this apprehension of and appreciation for food—sensory and spiritual and gastrointestinal—seems coincidental with what others call his hypochondria and what I have come to consider his rare antennae for the flavors of mortality, a keen aptitude for the taste of survival.

What I mean to say is that over sashimi at the Ikkyu (Tottenham Court Road near the Goodge Street Station), the talk will inevitably turn to the number of Japanese (just south of five hundred in the most recent tally) killed every year by the ingestion of a toxin-containing organ in an otherwise harmless (when properly skinned and eviscerated) puffer fish called fugu. Did the menu predestine the conversation? Once preparing an Umbrian dish of sausage and lentils, meant to replicate a specialty of the Trattoria Dal Francese, in Norcia, he asked what I knew about urinary tract infections, male sexual dysfunctions, inflammations of the colon and diverticuli, the prognostic implications of chronic flatus. Was it the sausage and lentils? I wondered. Was there a connection between foodstuffs and the fear of doom in Matthew's complex psychopathology? Why, for example, while precisely dicing the chives for inclusion in a garnish for rainbow trout, would the light-hearted chit-chat lurch from the morning's catch (from a trout pond in northern Michigan) to the manifold dangers of microsurgery. "One infinitesimal slip of the wrist," he said, "and you can't walk, or can't talk, or you'll drool for the rest of your miserable life." And once, over what I believe to be the hemisphere's finest presentation of lobster at Manuel DiLucia's in Corbally, near my cottage in Clare, Matthew began to question me on deaths by misadventure, especially falling from severe heights. In particular he wanted to know if any forensic evidence could be cited in support of his hope that such deaths occurred somewhere between the top and bottom of the fall rather than as a result of the ultimate impact of the fall itself.

I have long thought it my professional duty, when questioned by someone of Matthew's sensibilities, to either give the true answer when it is known to me, or to suggest a source in the topical literature where such an answer might be found, or, failing either of these, to make something up.

In accordance with which personal maxim, I made mention to Matthew of a highly regarded theory, first proffered by a student of C. G. Jung's, that the presence of an overwhelming existential threat to the organism produces glandular secretions and other biochemical adaptations that occlude the cerebral synapse through which the business of nerve cells is, in the norm, conducted. This psychobiological response amounts to none other than a kind of coma from which, depending on the distance of the fall, the victim either awakens with broken but reparable bones in the nearest emergency ward or does not awaken at all. In either event, it could be fairly stated, your man would never know what hit him or, in this case—since between the faller and the fallen on, the former seems the more proactive—what he hit.

Matthew, transfixed by my testimony, allowed himself a taste of the lobster, a bit of brown bread and a sup of Puligni-Montrachet. Rosemary, for the Sweeneys had come to West Clare *en famille*, assisted the children with the cracking of shells and the choice of utensils. I could see in her eyes the blue patience of the saintly who live with writers of Matthew's stripe—a depth of comisery and understanding I've seen, alas, in my own darling Mary's eyes. I thought we might ease our way toward orthodontics or adolescence or the shape of the universe or any of several more inclusive topics. But aflicker in Matthew's eyes I could see uncertainty, insatiety, the lingering remnant of the reasonable doubt that has set free many a guilty man, and saved a few of the blameless, too.

Was it because Manuel DiLucia's (Our host was a descendant of one of the few survivors of the Spanish Armada run aground off the West Clare coast in a storm centuries ago. Most of those who crawled ashore, it is reported, were slaughtered by the native Irish.) was perched on a cliff overlooking Kilkee and the rugged coastline southwest to Loop Head? Were these treacherous precipices reminiscent, I wondered, of Matthew's boyhood near Malin Head, the northernmost outpost of Ireland, where the land rises half a mile above the sea? I was reminded of my countryman, Edgar Allen Poe, whose "imp of the perverse" was the name he gave to that voice in all of us which, on the brink of such a deadly height, says "Jump!" Was it Poe who held that in everything's creation is the kernel of its own destruction? Or Melville? My memory was foggy on these points with which Matthew no less might readily agree.

I thought maybe some empirical evidence, albeit gathered from my own narrow studies, might satisfy his current hunger. I told him of a man I once embalmed, a worker in a scrap metal and salvage yard, on whom a car had fallen, fatally. No doubt, someone's plummet from a great height would have been more illustrative but by ordinance the tallest building in Milford is three stories, so that death by nosedive is rare around here. So this was no Icarus, no man fallen from the sky. Rather this was a man on whom the sky had fallen, in the form of a '67 Mustang convertible, itself the victim of a head-on collision. Both the Mustang and the huge magnetic disc that held it dropped on the poor fellow when the giant crane from which they hung gave way on account of a thing called metal "fatigue." The victim of the tragedy was rummaging for hubcaps in a heap below—in the wrong place at the wrong time, to be sure.

Few comforts can be wrung from such events. No compensation from the insurance carrier, no lofty talk in praise of the dead, nor fellow feeling for those left behind can right the wrongness of such happenings. It was, in the words of my eldest son who brought the body back from the county morgue, "a bad thing."

Something in the look on Matthew's face told me that further detail on the dead man's circumstances, or family, were hardly called for, so completely had Matthew already identified with this hapless client, killed one weekday by the falling sky.

But what I thought I ought to tell my friend was this, that for all the damage done, and it was considerable—we're talking several tons here from maybe a hundred feet—the look on your man's face was serenity itself, a peace that proclaimed nothing so loudly as his ignorance of or concurrence with the

Unknown Forces that dropped this car on him. There was, among the wounds and contusions and fractures and traumas, an aspect of the man's visage that looked like he wanted to tell us *Have a nice day!* And though I thought it might be a source of encouragement to his mother and his significant other, they pretty much had their mind set on a closed casket.

Now brimming with sympathy for his fellow pilgrim, his fellow traveler through this vale of tears, Sweeney looked westward through the window where the sun was declining into the North Atlantic on the brink of which his wife and children, for Rosemary had tactfully removed them for "some fresh air," stood silhouetted by the evening light. Gulls hovered in the updraft at the cliffs'-edge, overhead them. The lights of small boats bound for the bay mingled with the light of early stars.

I ordered him a snifter of brandy.

If life is like a box of chocolates, no less should be said for a lobster dinner. There are lessons for the living to be learned from it. Among the ones I've learned are these: Some of us taste and some of us savor. For some it's a chore, for others, a treat. Some eat and run and some eat and wonder. Some of it's hunted, some is gathered. Some is slaughtered, some we reap. Some of it's fresh and some is fermented. Some of it's living, some of it's dead. All of our hungers are not the same.

After years of dining with Matthew Sweeney, after years of trading poems, stories, recipes, and friends, I have come to believe that what he sensed as a baby, what he knew as a boyo, what he knows as a man is that we die. On this account he is absolutely right. If his wariness seems acute, intense, at times neurotic, it could just as easily be called a gift.

Perhaps he sees the ghost in the mirror. Or feels the chill in every touch. Perhaps he hears the imp more clearly. Or sniffs the rotting with the sweet.

Maybe it's only his taste buds are better for the seed in his being of his ceasing to be.

All Hallows' Eve

I wanted to know the day I would die. It seemed a useful bit of information for handicapping insurance policies, timing regrets, tendering farewells to former lovers. I wanted some precision in the calculation—if not the day, then possibly the age at which I'd cease to be, at least so far as those around me were concerned.

The gene-pool was unclear on this. The men in the family had all died of hearts: congested, infarcted, occluded, spent—all of their ends had proceeded from their chests, mostly in their sixties. My mother's father, a great bingy man, died in my childhood, a narrow memory now of a bald man telling bear stories. He'd grown up in Michigan's upper peninsula around the turn of the twentieth century, come downstate for an education at Ann Arbor, and married, as my grandmother told it, the first woman who'd have him. But Pat O'Hara, though he lived the civilized life in southeastern lower Michigan ever after, would leave his bride, Marvel Grace, every autumn for a month and return to the UP where he'd drink and hunt and fish and make up the stories I remember him telling us, of being treed by bears and wolves and other wildlife we would never see. And though Pat died at age sixty-two, Marvel, my grandmother, lived on after him for nearly thirty years until a stroke left her cognizant but bedfast for eight months of withering to death at age ninety. I was thirty-five the year she died and beginning to think of myself as mortal.

My father's father died, likewise, of a heart attack, when I was sixteen. I remember the call at the bowling alley where I worked. He was sixty-four. He'd driven up to Frankenmuth with the missus for dinner at Zehnder's Famous Chicken Dinners—two and a half hours north of Detroit. On the way home, the pain started shooting down his left arm. He thought it might be the gravy or the chicken livers. Back home, they called the doctor, the fire department, the priest, and my father. All were at the bedside where he sat upright in his suspenders and undershirt while the doctor examined him and the priest nodded assurances to my grandmother and the firemen stood ready with oxygen tanks—an assemblage resembling a Rockwell print that might have been titled: "The Good Death." My father, just turned forty, probably felt wary and helpless. I'm only guessing. Anyway, the doctor pressed the stethoscope in the usual places and after considerable silence pronounced his diagnosis: "Eddie, I can't find a thing wrong with you." Whereupon Eddie, ever contentious, slumped to the floor, turned purple, and died in an instant, proving for all in attendance, once and for all, the fallibility of modern medicine, and the changeability of life in general.

Because my father owned a funeral home, it fell to my brother Dan and me to dress Pop Lynch and casket him—the first of my people I ever tended to professionally. I can't remember now if my father simply asked if we would or insisted or offered us the opportunity. But I remember feeling, immediately, relieved that I could do something, anything, to help.

Still, I subtracted my years from his years and began to think of the future as finite—the first among those facts of life that look like arithmetic.

Gramma Lynch, like Nana O'Hara, lived on until she was ninety. The decades of their concurrent widowhoods became, for me, a series of Sundays and Christmases and Fourths of July when we'd find them on the patio or at the kitchen table, tippling their Canadian whiskey and water, arguing politics and religion and correcting the English of their grandchildren. Gramma Lynch was Republican, practical, younger by ten years and only Catholic by conversion. A Methodist by rearing, she regarded the clergy as circuit riders and opportunists, passers-by in the life of faith. She mistrusted the celibacy and the celebrity of priests and ate meat on Fridays. She lived within her means, was slow to criticize, and temperate but genuine when it came to praise. Nana was a Democrat, a member of the teachers' union, Catholic in the devout and idolatrous style of the Irish, scrupulous, full of etiquette, eloquent and extravagant in praise and shaming. Their arguments were brilliant, better than any theater. Where Nana used language as a weapon, Gramma used silence. If Nana spouted certainty, Gramma whispered reasonable doubt. Nana punctuated with the pointed finger, Gramma with the arched eyebrow. No one won. That they lived long lives and that I lived mine in earshot of their quarrels was, I can only say, a gift. They are buried now in different sections of the same cemetery, beside the men they outlived by years and years. I remember their obsequies: prim and proper and full of high talk—like them.

My grandmothers were powerful women—mighty in ways I see in their granddaughters and great-granddaughters. Neither ever suffered any problem she could not give a name to. There was no mention of silence in need of breaking. There was, to be sure, little silence at all. A division of labor, typical of their generation, did not require an abdication of power. If they earned sixty-three cents to their husbands' dollar, they got to live another decade or two or three on their dead men's pension or social security. If their husbands had political and financial and large muscle advantage, the women had emotional and spiritual and demographic comeuppance. The realization that God could be female required the consideration that the Devil could be also. My grandmothers were inclined to leave well enough alone. For most women, of course, things were just not that well enough. The world as they knew it was about to change.

My mother and I shared that portion of the century that saw gender gaps begin to open and close and open again. Women gave up homemaking in favor of house payments, lobbied for political and fiscal parity, and began to die of the heart attacks, car wrecks, and gastrointestinal disorders their menfolk had always died of, younger and better insured than their mothers before them. Even their suicides, formerly dainty, ladylike endeavors involving pills and gas stoves and other hushed methods, became more assertive and noisy—pistols first, then shotguns. The silence was broken. In some odd quarters, this was counted as progress.

A traditionalist in most matters of life, my mother was, nonetheless, ahead of her time when it came to death, dying twenty-eight months before my father, when she was sixty-five, of a cancer that took her voice away.

So neither gender nor gene pool was much of a predictor. I began to look elsewhere for some answers.

I had this theory. It was based loosely on the unremarkable observation that the old are always looking back with longing while the young, with the same longing, look ahead. One man remembers what the other imagines. I think the theory holds for women, too. The vision of pleasure in the arms of the beloved, or of triumph after great effort, of safety snatched from the hold of peril, or of comfort after long struggle—whether produced by memory or expectation, age or youth, the ache is the same, and so is the vision.

My theory held that we could calculate the precise midpoint of life by an application of these none too ponderous truths. And knowing the precise midpoint would, of course, give me the Thing Most Unknown: the day I would die. Knowing the middle, the end could be known. It was algebra: x's and equal signs, a's plus b's.

If the past is a province the aged revisit and the future is one that the child dreams, birth and death are the oceans that bound them. And midlife is the moment between them, that frontier when its seems as if we could go either way, when our view is as good on either side. We are filled less with longing than with wonder. We fear less and worry more. These are only a few of the symptoms. The old write memoirs, the young do resumés. In midlife we keep a kind of diary that always begins with a discussion of the weather. The present is where we live, equidistant from our birth and death. We find our current spouse as compelling as the memory of our first lover or our fantasies about the tight asses and flat bellies in the magazine ads for undergarments.

There is about midlife a kind of balance, equilibrium—neither pushed by youth nor shoved by age: we float, momentarily released from the gravity of time. We see our history and future clearly. We sleep well, dream in all tenses, wake ready and able.

Think of it, I would say to anyone who'd listen in my drinking days, think of it as America. You emerge from the broken water of the womb like your forebears on Ellis Island. The language is unknown to you. You don't understand the food, the customs. You're willing but unable to work. You need someone to show you the ropes. In the best of cases your parents will do this. You head west, dreaming of gold and glamour and your future. Somewhere in the Poconos you meet a girl. You pick up some savvy and street smarts in Ohio. Maybe you detour to the quick comforts of Memphis or New Orleans, or northward to fish the salmon run in Michigan, but you never stray far or very long from the urgent westward intention of youth. California is where gold and memorable sex are. California is Hollywood and a City of Angels. It is where, when you get there, you will belong.

Maybe, when you cross the river in St. Louis, the girl you first took up with in Pennsylvania begins to seem a little backward for such a trendy fellow as yourself. Or maybe she dumps you for a guy from the old neighborhood or some slick talker from the Rockies with money. Good riddance is the thing you say and travel lightly, never looking back. In Vegas you get a little crazy, sleep around, buy a convertible, take your losses, drive out in the desert where it occurs to you you're your own worst enemy. You think of the gang from the old neighborhood, your elders are dying now or are dead. You keep remembering the flesh of your first lover. You make a lot of long-distance calls. For the first time in your life, you slow your pace, taking your time through the Grand Canyon, beginning a lot of sentences with *when I was your age* and *twenty or thirty years back now*. There are days so beautiful you regret you will die.

When the desert or the mountains or the wilderness doesn't kill you, you find yourself in California. Nothing seems as important as it once did. You mention to anyone who will listen that it was never the destination, after all. It was where you came from and the going there. Someone, meaning to be helpful, says you can never go home again. If all goes well at this point, you will take your leave easily, falling of the long dock in Santa Barbara, remembered by your children and their children, who grieve you all across the continent of age.

Of course, the middle of your life was back in Kansas where the horizon seemed endless on either side. You can see for miles, the stars come out, you are balanced between your infancy and decrepitude, your Bronx and Santa Barbara, your beginning and your end; balanced by your equal vision of what's behind you and before you, the done deals and possibilities. Upright, at ease in your skin: Kansas. It only lasts a moment. When you recognize the terrain, you are in the middle. Double your age for the day you will die. If it happens when you're twenty, figure on forty. If you're forty when it happens, count your blessings, save more, pick names for great-grandchildren. It's a simple theory, really. Algebra, history, geography, nothing fancy.

I was eighteen when this theory came to me. I was considering options for my future. I was a college student, not so much dodging the draft as trying to ignore it. Emblematic of the age was that one's prospects for Vietnam—as synonymous with death as cancer was, still is—were determined by a lottery, the brainchild of the Nixon administration. The days of the year were pulled from a hat—the order in which they were pulled would be the order in which new soldiers were called to serve. The issue of your mortality was linked to the day of your birth. I was playing Hearts in the student union when they drew the numbers. Mine turned out to be 254. It was widely figured they'd never draft past number 150. I was to be spared. I had a future. I wanted to be a poet. I had discovered Yeats. I wanted to be Simon and Garfunkel. I could play the guitar. I considered teaching, briefly. I thought getting my license as a funeral director would be no bad thing, in case I didn't get a record contract or a Pulitzer. I was utterly preoccupied with the first person singular.

About the only thing I knew for sure about my future was that I wanted to spend a good portion of it in the embrace of Johanna Berti, or someone like her. She had recently disabused me of years of blissless ignorance the nuns and Christian Brothers had labored to maintain. For these, the only good body was a dead body: Christ's. St. Stephen's, St. Sebastian, the poor bastard, St. Dorothy, Virgin and Martyr, patroness of gardeners. In parochial school of the fifties and sixties, love and death were inexorably connected. Passion meant a slow death for a good cause. Our schoolrooms and psyches were galleries of crucifixions, martyrdoms, agonies in the garden, ecstasies of unspecified origins, all for the sake of love. Johanna, herself a good Catholic and Italian who bore more than a passing resemblance to St. Catherine de Ricci, the correspondent of St. Philip Neri, fixed all of that in the ordinary way—by extending the available welcomes of one body to another. My future seemed abundant and shapeless.

I was living in my father's funeral home at the time. Not the one I own and operate now, but an earlier version. I took death calls at night and went on removals. One night a woman called to say her son had "taken his own life" and was now at the county medical examiner's where they would be doing an autopsy in the morning and would we go then and pick him up. When I got him back to the funeral home and unwrapped him, I was amazed at the carnage. The T-shaped incision on his chest was no surprise—the standard thoracic autopsy. But unwrapping his head from the plastic bag the morgue-men had wrapped it in, I found a face unimaginably reconfigured. There were entire parts of his cranium simply missing. He'd gotten a little liquored up and gone to the home of his ex-girlfriend. Rumor was she had broken up with him a week or two earlier and he had moped around the edges of her life in a way we would call "stalking" nowadays. He drank too much. He went to her house where he pleaded with her to take him back. Of course, she wouldn't, couldn't, wanted to be "just friends," etc . . ., and so he broke in, ran up to her parents' bedroom, where he took the deer rifle from her father's closet, lay on the bed with the muzzle in his mouth, and pulled the trigger with his big toe. It was, according to the ex-girlfriend, "a remarkable gesture."

As I considered the gesture on the table before me, it struck me, he looked ridiculous. His face had been split in two by the force of the blast, just above the bridge of his nose. He looked like a melon dropped from the cart, a pumpkin vandalized by neighbor boys. The back of his head simply wasn't. Here was a young man who had killed himself, remarkably, to deliver a message to a woman he wanted to remember him. No doubt she does. I certainly do. But the message itself seemed inconsequential, purposefully vague. Did he want to be dead forever or only absent from the pain? "I wanted to die" is all it seemed to say clearly. "Oh" is what the rest of us say.

But fixed in my remembrance is the way one eye looked eastward and one eye west; a perspective accomplished by the division of his face by force of arms. It seemed that this vantage would give a balanced vision: an eye on the future and an eye on the past. A circumspection by which where he'd been and where he was going melded into balance. But in the case before me, it was clear, vision was impossible. He was dead. So a sub-theory of the first I began to develop was that balance and vision could not be forced. Violence was not the way to vision. Guns wouldn't work for this. It had to be grown into, inhabited the way the wood does trees. The fellow before me on the porcelain table had achieved perspective at the expense of vision, vantage at the expense of life itself. He looked ridiculous and terribly damaged. And ever since, though I have felt helpless, and hopeless, and murderous, and grieved, I have never had, that I can remember, a suicidal moment in my life.

Walking upright between the past and future, a tightrope walk across our times, became, for me, a way of living: trying to maintain a balance between the competing gravities of birth and death, hope and regret, sex and mortality, love and grief, all those opposites or nearly opposites that become, after a while, the rocks and hard places, synonymous forces between which we navigate, like salmon balanced in the current, damned some times if we do or don't.

It happened for me one night some years ago. Is it needless to say we had just made love? She lay smoking a cigarette beside me. I was propped on my elbows looking out of the window. The night was Tuesday and moonlit, the end of October, All

Hallows' Eve. We had buried my mother that morning. We'd stood in the gray midmorning at Holy Sepulchre watching the casket go into its vault, a company of the brokenhearted at the death of a good woman, dead of cancer, her body buried under the din of priests and leaf fall and the sad drone of pipers. It had been a long day. I was trying to remember my mother's voice. The tumor had taken it from her in doses. I was beginning to panic because I'd never hear her voice again, the soft contralto, full of wisdom and the acoustics of safety.

And there, for a moment, I could see it all that night. Between the dead body of the woman who had given me life and the lithe body of the woman who made me feel alive, I had a glimpse of my history back to my birth and a glimpse of the future that would end in my death.

And the life on either side of that moment was nothing but heartache and affection, romance and hurt, laughter and weeping, wakes and leavetakings, lovemaking and joys—the horizontal mysteries among a landscape that looked like Kansas. I was overwhelmed with grief and desire. Grief for the mother that birthed me, desire for the woman beside me unto death. In such a moment the past loses its pull, the future its fear.

I was forty-one that October. And there are times, still, I'm tempted to reckon the math of it, or the geography, or the algebra or biology—to coax life's facts into some paradigm that suits, to say it's just like this or it's just like that. But since that night, afloat between the known affections of women who've loved me, I have lost my taste for numbers and easy models. Life's sciences have more to teach me still.

Revision and prediction seem like wastes of time. As much as I'd like to have a handle on the past and future, the moment I live in is the one I have. Here is how the moment instructs me: clouds float in front of the moon's face, lights flicker in the carved heads of pumpkins, leaves rise in the wind at random, saints go nameless, love comforts, souls sing beyond the reach of bodies.

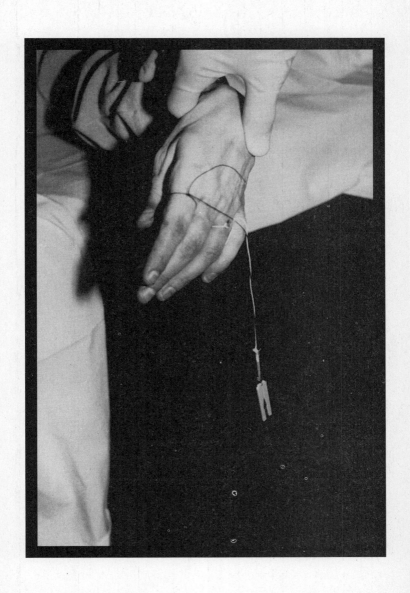

Uncle Eddie, Inc.

Instead of having "answers" on a math test,
they should just call them "impressions," and
if you got a different "impression," so what,
can't we all be brothers?

—JACK HANDY, *DEEP THOUGHTS*

Uncle Eddie needed an 800 number. His sideline in the suicide clean-up trade was going gangbusters. Business was booming. They were dropping like flies. He needed a separate line, a logo, a slogan, and magnetic business cards. I was touched that he would come to me, his much elder brother, for free advice.

"Whadaya think about 1-800-SUICIDE? Too morbid? Too direct?"

"Well, Ed . . ."

"Or 1-800-TRIPLE S? You know. For *Specialized Sanitation Services?*"

In his heart of hearts he had hopes that Triple S—for *Specialized Sanitation Services*—would become as widely recognized as Triple A had for the Automobile Association of America, or WWW for the World Wide Web, or Triple X for a type of film, the watching of which, Uncle Eddie always said, aroused his pride in First Amendment Rights.

Perhaps his services were a little *too* specialized—known only to local and state law enforcement agencies and county medical examiners and funeral homes; only needed by the families and landlords of the messy dead. Indoor suicides, homicides, household accidents, or natural deaths undetected in a timely fashion—these were the exceptional cases that often required the specialized sanitation services that Uncle Eddie and his staff at Triple S—his wife, his golfing buddy, and his golfing buddy's wife—stood ever ready to provide for reasonable fees most often covered by the Homeowner's Policy. If not the sort of thing you'd find in the yellow pages, still, tough work that someone had to do.

"Maybe you should just play whatever numbers come up Ed. Maybe ask for something that ends in zeros."

At this Uncle Eddie's visage changed—adopting the distant and bedazzled gape of the ancient Mayan perplexed by the delicate mysteries of nothingness.

Years ago I would do it for nothing. I'd only been in town a matter of months when the chief of police then, a fellow Rotarian, called the funeral home in the middle of the night to ask if we had anyone on the staff who took care of "the messes . . . you know, the really bad ones."

"We've had a bad one over here on Highland Road. You're getting the body, but he's gone to the morgue. I just can't let his family back in the house until something's done with it. Really bad."

I wondered if the Chief imagined a door in the funeral home marked BAD ONES behind which specialists in "messes" waited for calls.

"Well, we don't have anyone in particular, Chief, but I'll be over and I'll try Wes," referring to Wesley Rice, our chief embalmer, a man from the old school who was well used to emergencies in the dark.

It seems the late mortgagee of the split-level home on Highland Road had grown weary of his wife's ongoing affair with the chiropractor for whom she worked. Details of the tryst were sketchy, the Chief said. It had all started with an "adjustment." Push had apparently come to shove.

"Yep," he said. "The eternal triangle." He spit on the sidewalk in front of the house. "She's taken the kids and gone to her sister's place. Won't come back until it's clean."

The Chief had been able to piece it together, from physical evidence and the widow's understandably agitated testimony. The cuckholded householder had sat up drinking after his wife had gone to bed, announcing her intention to put spongy rollers in her hair. This had become an intimate code that meant to him she did not want to have sex with him but wanted to look good for the boss tomorrow. He'd finished the bottle of Dunphy's Irish and raided her stash of Valium, then gone to the drawer where the Black & Decker electric carving knife was kept between Easters and Thanksgivings and Christmases. He'd plugged it into the wall socket on his side of the bed, locked his jaw against any utterance and, laying down beside her, applied the humming knife to his throat, severing his two ascending carotid arteries and jugular veins and making it half through his esophagus before he released his hold on the knife's trigger. It had not been his coming to bed, nor the buzz of the knife, nor any sound he'd made, if, indeed, he'd made any, that woke her. Rather, it was the warmth of his blood, which gushed from his severed blood vessels halfway up the master bedroom wall and soaked her and her spongy rollers and saturated the bed linens and mattress and box springs and puddled in the carpet beneath the bed that woke her wondering was it just a dream.

Wes and I worked until daybreak. We removed the carpet and the mattress and box springs, tossed out the pile of magazines under the bed—soft porn and hunting and truck magazines on his side, catalogues and *Cosmopolitan*'s on hers. We soaked the knickknacks on the dresser in a commercial cleaning solution, wiped the plastic surfaces that had red dots of blood: the phone the clock radio, the color TV. Then we painted the room, except for the ceiling, with paint we found in the basement. Where the blood had soaked through the carpet and padding and left a stain on the hardwood floor, we scrubbed for a while, then left a towel saturated with bleach on it. We left then.

Wes, after much suturing and the use of a turtleneck sweater, was able to predict the possibility of an open casket, though nothing could be done about the dead man's mouth, which was clenched in the way you see in the movies when they give the wounded hero a bottle of hooch and a bit of leather to chew before they remove the bullet or the leg that the bullet was shot into.

The poor client looked, as a cousin several times removed remarked, "determined."

This is the part I have always admired—the determination, the pure resolve, to do one's self such massive and irreparable damage, which is the distinguishing element of all successful suicides. It distinguishes the true killer from the occasionally suicidal. Who among us in our right minds hasn't several times in the course of life yearned for the comforts of absence and non-being. But there is a subtle and important difference between those of us who'd rather not be alive tomorrow— incomplete homework, biopsy results, romantic reversals, pregnancy tests—and those of us who want to be dead, tomorrow and the day after and forever. The latter is the exception, the former, the rule.

This holds true for homicide as well as suicide. Indeed, my own neuroses tend toward the aggressive rather than the depressive disorders—toward the destruction of others and away from the destruction of self since I, like most funeral directors, nurse a fantasy in which I am the last man on the face of the earth having discharged my sad and profitable duties of burying everyone else, at which point I will be assumed into any available heaven with all my bills paid for the first time in my life. Most of us have, often times, if only momentarily, hungered for someone to fall off the planet. Former spouses, dental hygienists, government employees, fellow commuters at rush hour, teenagers, telemarketers, TV preachers, in-laws, parents, perfect strangers (and who among us isn't one of these) have all been the objects of homicidal scorn. But most of us will not be killers because we understand the difference between being angry enough to kill and being a killer.

Still, the impulse to turn our pain outward is a sibling to the impulse to turn it on ourselves. Whether we are always to blame or never to blame, we are still the center of a hurtsome universe. Homicide and suicide are verses of the same sad tune, close cousins of the one pathology.

To kill another of one's own species—be it one's "self" or one's "other"—calls for true resolve and a deadly silence, however momentary, of all the voices raised to the contrary. Of course, many of the voices are institutional. Governments pass laws that make it illegal to murder one's self or another. Religions cite texts that proclaim it immoral and unforgivable. Life, they argue, is sacred, in every one of its human incarnations. It's God's to give and God's to take away. Others extend such protections to endangered species, whales and snail-darters, owls and elm trees. This is the province of politicos and theologians. There are, notably, civil and ecclesiastical exceptions to these rules—hence, Holy Wars and executions. Suicides and homicides in the name of God or Justice or Mercy or Self-Defense are acceptable deviations from the norm.

But the noisier voices are our own, the elements of the self—psychological, biological, spiritual, social, intellectual. Free of flag and icon, each still argues against its end. As anyone who has swatted a wasp, or caught a fish, or shot an animal, or sat with the dying of our own kind knows, life—at a cellular level—rages against the dying of the light. Something in us argues, "Don't!"

Post mortem caloricity, they taught us in mortuary school, was the name for the way the body warms immediately after death occurs. The cells keep dividing, metabolizing, exchanging oxygen and protein, doing their accustomed work. With no exhaust system—breathing, sweating, weeping, farting—the system overheats. The cells shut down. Punch the clock. Call it a day. Then the dead body cools to room temperature, nearly thirty degrees cooler than the rest of us, accounting for one of our most frequently asked questions—why is it cold?

So there is a difference, an important difference, between when we die to our stethoscopes and encephalograms: *somatic* death; when we die to our nerve ends and molecules: *metabolic* death; and when we die to those around us—grandchildren and creditors, siblings and neighbors—an end we might call our *social* death.

In the same way birth has its degrees—from conception (metabolic) to viability (somatic) to naming or baptism or initiation (social). The order in which these deaths and these births happen is important, and historically we've shown a preference for the order I've outlined them in—our readiness and willingness to accept someone's new life or new death and its implications for ourselves, following by hours or days or weeks or years, either their ability or their refusal to produce what we call "vital signs." We do not baptize or name until we are reasonably certain the child will live and, as technology has increased viability, we name and baptize our babies younger and younger. Likewise, we do not bury until we are reasonably certain a person is dead (the fear of live burial is an ancient one), and most rituals follow an effort to "wake" the alleged decedant—just to be sure.

Funerals, in every culture and history, have sought to nudge the bereaved toward an acceptance of The Facts just as baptisms or their equivalents have sought to do the same for the fecund. And the rituals surrounding births and deaths provide a paradigm for the safe and sane management of the implications of a new dead body on the floor or a new live one.

Accordingly, ceremonial, symbolic, and practical consider-
ations have always been addressed by such rituals. They address
the needs of living and dead, newborn and parents. At one end
of life the community declares *It's alive, it stinks, we'd better do
something*. At the other end we echo, *It's dead, it stinks, we'd better do something*. And ever since we emerged from the cosmos,
garden, or the primordial ooze, we have called it Nature's
Way or God's Will or The Great Mandala or The Facts of Life:
we are born, we die; we love and grieve; we breed and disappear. And whether God created nature or Nature created god,
the natural and godly death is unwelcome while the natural
and godly birth is a joy. Of course, there is a degree of ambivalence about both events. No birth is entirely wonderful or free
of worries and no death is entirely awful, without its blessings
and consolations. We may tolerate it, accept it, regard it as
appropriate or merciful or timely. Nonetheless, until just
lately, birth has been the bundle of joy, the miracle of life; and
death has been the unwelcome guest—the dark angel, the
grim reaper, the thief in the night, the son of a bitch.

When the order is disturbed, it seems unnatural. We are left
with an anomaly. Our sense of timing is offended. Thus, when
social death precedes somatic death we end up with someone
buried alive. Or its latter day equivalent: stashed in a nursing
home, out of the loop, in every way but arterially, out of cir-
culation. We'd rather Nature had taken a course that got them
out of life just slightly before we were ready to be quit of
them. We often blame medical science, and its new technologies, for separating us from our nature. Let go, we say. Get out
of the way. Let Nature take its course, however imperfect the
outcomes might be.

At the other end of life, however, we are less willing to trust
in Nature's Way or God's Will or whatever we call it when
we're not in charge. We embrace with few questions a technology that allows us to plan, control, subvert, abort, design,
and decide on gender, hair color, and sexual preference. A

somatic birth that precedes a social birth, up until lately the only option, is reckoned an accident, an outrage, a surprise— "oops" we say, to an unplanned pregnancy. Unwilling to let go or get out of the way or let Nature take its course, we lobby for more and more "options."

Thus, what has always seemed offensive about suicide—that it seemed to subvert Nature's intentions, or God's intentions, whomever's in charge—is rendered acceptable, indeed, preferable, at the other end of life, by the user-friendly doctrines of Control and Choice (as in birth control and reproductive choice), which seem to suggest that, when we can, we should play God or fool Mother Nature.

Still, what offends us about homicide—even those sanctioned by the Church or the State—is that it too disrupts the order. "Life has Meaning and Value" the signs read that march against wars and hangings, abortions and euthanasia. But those who uphold the state's rights to make war and execute criminals often decry the right to "Choice" or "Death with Dignity." Just as those who uphold abortion rights and the right to die turn out in droves against Vietnam, the Gulf War, the lethal injection of a serial killer.

More subtle and more troubling are the truths that wars have been waged for greed and glory rather than humanitarian causes, abortion has been used in the service of sexist, racist, and classist agendas, and euthanasia has been, at times, the thin veil over genocide, abuse, neglect, and homicide. All of our "choices" have not been good ones.

Thus, the great divisions of the last half century and the next half century seem based on the contemplation of Life and Death: when one becomes the other and under whose agency. The advance of our technology is coincidental with the loss of our appetite for ethical questions that ought to attend the implications of these new powers. We have blurred the borders between being and ceasing to be by a technology that can tell us How It Works but not What It Means. Nor do we trust our instincts anymore. If we sense something is Wrong, we are embarrassed to say so, just as we are when we sense it is Right. In the name of diversity, any idea is regarded as worthy as any other; any nonsense is entitled to a forum, a full hearing, and equal time. Reality is customized to fit the person or the situation. There is *your* reality and *my* reality, the truth as *they* see it, but what is real and true for us all eludes us. We frame our personal questions in terms of the legal and illegal, politically correct or incorrect, function or dysfunction, how it impacts our self-esteem, or puts us in touch with our feelings, or bodes for the next election or millage vote or how the markets will respond. And while business of all sorts can be conducted this way to the relative advantage of all concerned, on the Big Questions, the Existential Concerns, the Life and Death Matters of *who is and who isn't to be*, what is called for are our best instincts, our finest intuitions, our clearest intellections and an honesty inspired by our participation, not in a party or a gender or a religion or a special interest or ethnicity, but by our participation in the human race.

And here, the dialogue seems oddly hushed. Is it possible we are just too busy, just don't care? Are we willing to leave it to the experts?

No member of my generation: that demographic aneurysm called the Baby Boom, should miss the hapless irony that the first generation to plan its parenthood, to manage and manipulate its fertility, may well be the first generation to have our deaths planned for us, our morality managed and manipulated by our own children, those who survived the gauntlet of our choices. Likewise, we can depend upon them to make their choices the way we've made ours: by convenience and expedience and five-year plans, efficiency and function and high performance, quality time and available resources. *Less*, we've always lied to them, is *more!* Maybe we shouldn't have fooled

Mother Nature. Maybe we just should have played whatever numbers came up, instead.

"What do you think about ball caps and windbreakers?" Uncle Eddie was thinking about uniforms.

"In dark, dark green, you know, it's all the rage. And three S's embroidered tastefully in gold? Inside a pyramid design? You know. Classic. Timeless. Very professional. Whaddaya think?"

I cautioned him about expenses and cash–flow. Better to start small. Get a few jobs under his belt, some money in the bank, and work up to full uniforms. "You've got to walk before you run," I said.

He'd been pushed to the limit by a rash of bad ones. A murder-suicide involving kitchenware and large-caliber handguns in an apartment complex south of town had been, for Triple S, a sad bonanza in terms of on-the-job training and accounts receivable. He'd already invested in gloves and face masks, protective goggles and disposable footwear for his staff. He'd leased a van, also in deep forest green, and outfitted it with buckets and mops and cleaning solutions. He'd purchased ozone machines for the removal of odors and had contracts and invoices printed up. He'd had training sessions with his staff, instructing them on the discreet discharge of their duties, the importance of team work, high standards of performance, the disposal of biohazards, the possibility of a Christmas party, bonuses, the avoidance of bloodborne pathogens and other exposures. He'd paid for their hepatitis B vaccinations. He'd given them beepers and name badges.

Like AIDS and alcoholism, suicide has a certain contagion. *Why?* is the question it always poses and when no sufficient answer is given, *Why not?* is what we ask rhetorically, trying to bring the outrage into the realm of the sensible. To make self killing "understandable," "forgivable," one need only see it as the last remarkable and fatal symptom of a life-threatening illness, a fatal disease—depression or melancholia. But to make it "permissible," legal, an inalienable right, we must argue against the absolute value of life. It must become "relative," "negotiable," a matter of opinion, open to various interpretations. We proclaim it an option—a matter of "choice." To be or not to be, becomes, like smoking or non-smoking, window or aisle seat, the choice of salad dressing or type of wine, a matter of individual taste, situation, and circumstance—answerable to public opinion, provincial ordinance, or political reality, perhaps, but no longer the province of Nature or Divinity.

We have done as much with the matter of birth and parenting, dividing ourselves into different teams—pro-Thisers or pro-Thaters—with no middle ground, as there seldom is in matters of life and death. The debate is controlled by the extremes, each side shouting answers and accusations over the heads of the people in between, who are kept from formulating questions by the din of the argument all around them. Each paints the other with a broader brush. Each has an arsenal of names and adjectives to deploy against the other side. No one listens. Everyone screams.

W*hy leave a mess? Call TRIPLE S!* is the slogan Uncle Eddie invented. He had it printed in 22-point Mead Bold gold letters on a dark green background along with his 800-number (1-800-668-4464), made into kitchen-magnet cards and mailed them out in batches by the half-dozen to police and fire stations, funeral homes, and the county morgues here in southeastern lower Michigan. He included a cover letter that made mention of his round-the-clock cellular dispatch, his willingness to work with insurance companies, his highly-trained and professional staff, his free on-site quotations. Key words like *body fluids, blood-borne pathogens, tissues, putrefaction, maggots*, intermingled with *disinfection, restoration, cleanliness*, and *discretion* to make the case for why they should call Specialized Sanitation Services, Inc.; at the bottom of which letterhead Uncle Eddie signed his name under which he typed out *Founder and President*.

Before he knew it the phone began to ring—once or twice a month at first, then once or twice a week. "They're dying to see me!" Uncle Eddie said. There was the occasional murder that called for his attention, or the old timers dead but undiscovered—one old man died on the floor of his bungalow in August and wasn't found for most of a month after which a floor sander and kerosene were added to Uncle Eddie's supplies. But for the most part Triple S relied on the grisly and violent homemade suicides, which erred on the side of excess and overkill, to cover the fixed costs of the enterprise.

After six months of bedrooms and bathtubs and basements, car trunks, hotel rooms, and offices, Uncle Eddie was dreaming of franchising and helicopters, to extend the coverage of Triple S, Inc.

It was June of 1990 when one of our local "characters" here in Oakland County, an unemployed pathologist and failed movie mogul, put Janet Adkins in his rusting minibus, drove her out to Groveland Township, a few miles north of here, then showed her the button on his "Thanatron"—a gizmo he'd rigged from garage-sale parts to give a lethal injection of potassium chloride: a suicide machine. She pushed the button. The machine worked. Machines do. Janet Adkins was taken to the county morgue where a thoracic and cranial autopsy was done. Jack Kevorkian was taken to the county jail, a floor above her in the same building. Then Janet was taken to the crematory at Evergreen Cemetery and burned into oblivion and Jack got his picture on the cover of *Time*. So everyone got what it was they wanted.

Except Uncle Eddie who was beside himself. "Who's this fellow Dr. Death?" he hollered. "And why is he trying to put me out of business?" The small blood vessels in his head were bulging. He was pointing at the story in the daily paper.

I told him it had nothing to do with Triple S. But my younger brother, ever the visionary, said it was a genuine threat. He went on to explain that tidy, bloodless, medically supervised and assisted suicides would make his Specialized Sanitation Services redundant, his mop and bucket crews as obsolete as typewriters or telegraphs. "The handwriting's on the wall," he sighed. "It's only a matter of time."

I told him not to lose hope. Surely Kevorkian would go to jail or to the asylum. Injecting poisons was against the law. Clearly, suicide was not medicinal, though it was powerfully effective against all pains: physical, spiritual, and psychological; it was more murderous than remedial. "Assisted suicide" like "holy war" is an oxymoronic romance that seeks to make killing sound like kindness or courtesy or a good cause. Folks would soon go back to the old trusted solo ways—pills, gas stoves, bridge abutments, firearms—which made up in raw individual tidings whatever they lacked in tidiness.

Recent history has proven me wrong, dead wrong, wrong again.

By the end of 1996 Jack had assisted in nearly fifty "medicides" and was the darling of the deathly set of euthanasists, do-it-yourselfers, and radical empiricists that keep homepages on the Internet you can access by searching under suicide. The DeathNet they call it. You can try this at home.

Uncle Eddie says it's not the suicide. We've always had that. It's the *assistance* that there is a market for. Janet Adkins didn't need the help. Not with the killing part. She had the physical resources to swallow pills, pull a trigger, start a car, turn on the gas stove and thus avail herself of traditional methods. She had the psychological resources to overcome her fear of dying, a fear like the fear of any unknown. She had the spiritual resources to understand that God or Whatever Is Out There would, by virtue of its job description, understand her. What she lacked was the voice to shout down her own voices that whispered to her the case for living—part nature part nurture, the voice that says to take life, however painful and imperfect, does damage to the rest of life. Dr. Jack with his half-baked rationality and his jerry-rigged contraption—his Thanatron— and his ethically neutered lexicon made Janet his *patient* and poison, the *treatment*, and what they were doing, *medicide*; proving yet again the modern axiom that the big lie is easier to sell than the small one. By all the equipment he made it seem that his assistance had to do with *method*. By the mid-afternoon in early June in north Oakland County, in the back of his van, it all must have seemed normal, natural, a right and entitlement, a matter of choice, protected by the Constitution, maybe someday worthy of public funding. "Have a nice trip," he had told her, after she had done her part, as if she were off to the Bahamas or the Berkshires.

That great minds think alike is not a certainty. While Jack Kevorkian pursued his immortality—gladdened by his attorney's suggestion that his name recognition fell just south of Santa Claus, pleased with the attention of talk show hosts and PBS—Uncle Eddie saw only an eventual failure, a new world order in which suicide was no more messy than dentistry, the end of the line for Triple S.

After three trials here in Oakland County failed to convict or restrain Dr. Kevorkian, after the county prosecutor was voted out of office for spending tax dollars bringing the doctor to court (Dr. Jack prepared a lethal injection for Elizabeth Mercz, age 59, of Cincinnati, on election day to signal his acceptance of the mandate the voters seemed to be giving him. He delivered her body to the hospital just after the polls had closed), and after two federal district courts had ruled in favor of assisted suicide and motions were brought to bring it to the Supreme Court, Uncle Eddie pulled the plug on Triple S. He boxed up the kitchen magnets and coffee mugs, the memo pads with his logo and slogan, the ball caps and windbreakers, laid off his staff and answering service and sold the van, and sent a letter, full of regrets, to the agencies that had formerly called him.

And sad as I was for Uncle Eddie, all that night I tossed and turned among gray images of suicides I'd known. The boy who went out in the woods and hung himself and wasn't found until hunting season. The man with cancer and a deer rifle who sat with the barrel under his chin considering his options for an hour, making his case to the video-cam, then pulled the trigger. How bits of his skull were wedged into the wormwood panelling. His wife would find them afterward, for months, and call me wondering what she should do. And why it was he never turned the camera off.

Or the pills and booze crowd, mostly women, who washed down handfuls of antidepressants with half bottle chasers of Absolut. How one got dressed up in her wedding gown and did the same damage with pink champagne, her careful hand-writing turning to scrawl: "I'm sorry. I love you. I'm in such pain. . . ." And the household poisonings, rat killers, drain openers, paint thinners, liquid bleach—how the bodies would come to us foaming tiny white bubbles from every orifice.

The girl who climbed up the water tower. We would have counted her an accident until the medical examiner found breaks and fractures from her hips to heels. "You fall head first," he said. "Feet first's a jump." *Multiple Injuries* he ruled it—*Suicide*. I remember that poor child's family—each of them wondering what it was they'd done or failed to do or could have, should have, might have, would have surely done if they'd only known whatever it was that drove her up and down. Damned if they did or if they didn't, they went their own ways after that, alone. Or the woman who holed up in her room with a hot plate and her toddlers and a gun for days before she let the children out with a note for their father; then she shot herself. He loved and hated her ever after. Or the friend of mine who lay between his Buick's dual exhausts and breathed and breathed till he was out of breath and at a loss to say exactly what it was went wrong. There were, of course, the usual theories. Overbearing parents. A loss of faith. Confusion over sexuality. His troublesome madness? Genius? Either way, he's long since gone. His wounded people, still hungry for answers, stumble after him, with the lameness that comes from a foot in the grave.

Each of these suffered a strain of the sickness, the sadness that lies to the one who has it—the one that says it will never get better, no safe harbor, no choice in the matter, no available kindness but to quit. It's the sickness that makes its victims listless, hopeless, helpless, lifeless as stones. It's the grim indifference I've seen in the eyes of my own darling son once that made me shiver—the sense that I've had since that he could do it. He has the hurt, the deafness, and blindness for it—the will, despite all that we know of love, to go that distance utterly alone: the determination I have always admired and I have always feared.

Unlike Janet Adkins from Portland, Oregon, or Linda Henslee from Beloit, Wisconsin, or Esther Cohan from Skokie, Illinois, or Catherine Andreyev from Pennsylvania or Ruth Neuman from Columbus, New Jersey, or Lona D. Jones from Cheser, Virginia, or Bette Lou Hamilton from Ohio or Patricia Cashman, Jonathan D. Grenz and Martha Jane Ruwart—all Californians—or dozens of others who made their ways across the country or the county line, still unable to take the final fatal steps alone. We call it helpful, here in Michigan, to give the gas, to slip the needle in.

Perhaps it is our *nature* to die, not our right. Maybe we have the *ability* to kill, to make things dead, even ourselves, but we haven't the right. And when we exercise that ability, in the name of God (as we have done in war), or of Justice (as we have done with capital punishment), or of Choice (as we have with abortion), we should have the good sense to recognize it for what it isn't: enlightenment, civilization, progress, mercy. Nor is it an inalienable right. It is, rather, a shame, a sadness, a peril from which no congress's legislation, no churchman's dispensation, no public opinion or conventional wisdom can ever deliver us. For if we live in a world where birth is suspect, where the value of life is relative, and death is welcomed and well regarded, we live in a world vastly more shameful, abundantly sadder, and ever more perilous than all the primitive generations of our species before us who were sufficiently civilized to fill with wonder at the birth of new life, dance with the living, and weep for the dead.

Is a suicide less a killing than a homicide? When the killer and the one killed are one and the same, does it mitigate the offense of killing? And while a suicide may successfully thumb a nose at the rest of us, and may be welcomed into whatever heavens are out there by whatever merciful gods there are, some things really should be done on one's own. For suicide to be a *sui*-cide (a killing of one's self by one's self) it really ought to be done without assistance, without license, and without a moral proxy or surrogate. Does the ability to end life on our own terms suggest the right to do so, anymore than my ability to piss on my neighbor's daylilies implies an inalienable right to do so?

Few people are drawn to the discussion of such things. The folks I have coffee with most mornings in town are not so much "for" Kevorkian as indifferent to him. It is a sample heavily weighted with males—retirees and attorneys and small businessmen. Maybe it is only a sign of the times. Even when, after the excitement of the trials was over, Dr. Jack started delivering bodies to local hospitals, in keeping, according to one forensic psychiatrist, with the profile of serial killers who kill and dump and who need increasing doses of risk and stimuli; even when former jurors began to voice doubts; even when Dr. Jack applied for a concealed weapons permit, no one seemed to be much bothered. Of course, the dead were almost exclusively women, none of them local, none of them known to us, none of them young enough to interest anyone.

The absence of outrage is an outrage itself.

I should say what it is I am not saying here. I am not saying that we may not kill ourselves. We may, of course. Free Will is the name we give to this. We can likewise refuse any and all treatment designed to prolong our life or prevent our death. Whole segments of the population will never have to endure these "extraordinary measures"—not by choice but by simple economy. We don't have to wait until we're dying to do this. We can begin today. Just say *No thank you.* Just say *Goodbye.* I am not saying that we won't go to Heaven, or Las Vegas or into the void on account of these decisions, whatever they are. Nor am I suggesting that we endure any pain for which there is a medicine or treatment.

I am not suggesting that the professionals in Medicine or Pastoral Care or Government or Business have done all they could for our frightened and needy and endangered species. That so many are living and dying without the most basic creature comforts and protections in a country that has them in abundance is a scandal and a scourge. We have been far too tolerant of pain and suffering when it isn't our own. We are far better at fixing parts than people, far better at saving souls than comforting sinners, far better at killing than caring for the wounded.

Nor have we amateurs been much better—we parents and spouses and siblings and friends, we sons and daughters—we turn from the dying of the ones we love, as if their dying made them strange, abandoning them to the clean hands of trained professionals who regard the unfixable human condition as a waste of precious and highly priced time.

Is it possible to assist the ones we love with their dying instead of assisting with their killing?

I pose these questions not because I have an answer but because it seems we are there again. The rape victim in the back alley with coat hanger for whom the courts legalized abortion now is the pain-wracked incapacitant, *in extremis,* gone past the point of pulling a trigger or taking a pill, half comatose with morphine, beyond all hope, pleading for his or her right to assistance with the suicide they never got around to. This image is not a fiction. People are living this way. They are the exceptions, the painful cases—maybe the pitiful five percent, like the five percent of abortions performed for rape or incest or the sake of the mother's life.

Is there a way to care for these needy people without declaring another open season, a general Right to Die or Right to Choice or Right to Assisted Suicide?

Are we obliged to resolve the issue of assisted suicide the way we have never managed to resolve the issue of abortion? Must we join our teams again, get out the placards and the megaphones?

On all sides of the issue of assisted suicide there are those who caution against comparisons to the abortion debate. They caution against confusing the issue when what they mean to say is that such comparisons confuse the politics and the special interests. The comparison, in fact, clarifies the issues—they are both about how the living define the value of life and the meaning of death and the relative worth of each. Both issues are about borders and boundaries and "being" itself. And they both are about money and politics and special interests and the people who make their living off divisions in the citizenry. Assisted suicide and abortion are as near to mirror images of the same existential concerns as life in this century will provide. And if a review of the last quarter century living with safe and legal abortion does not tell us exactly how to settle the current debate, it surely tells us how we shouldn't.

Left to the courts, we'll get a late-century version of *Roe v. Wade*—a half-baked contraption of a court decision that has utterly divided people of goodwill and careful thought on both sides of the issue of abortion and turned them into para-legals, pseudo-litigants, armchair lobbyists, and dangerous zealots. "Why," as one supreme court justice has already asked, apparently learning from past mistakes, "would you want to leave the decision in the hands of nine attorneys?"

Left to chance, if we cower from the difficult issues, we get Kevorkian or a variation on his pathological if oddly cartoonish theme. Maybe a new and improved version of Triple S? But this time, maybe *Suicide Support & Supply*. The logo still works, the slogan holds: *Don't leave a mess call TRIPLE S!* The kitchen magnets could be mass mailed to nursing homes, retirement villages, homeless and battered spouse shelters, support groups for Alzheimers and multiple sclerosis and muscular dystrophy and Lou Gehrig's Disease. Word would get around. Why should Kevorkian have a corner on the market? And why only pathologists or doctors? Why not the clergy, why not academics, why not tradespeople and farmers and retired politicians and the press? They all know misery when they see it. They all know what it takes to kill. When it comes to killing and to mercy, what makes M.D.'s more qualified than D.O.'s Ph.D.'s, C.P.A.'s, M.B.A.'s or S.O.B.'s? If someone's going to assist you, after all, in your one and only suicide, oughtn't you to have, at least, a choice? Wouldn't you rather a priest than a proctologist? Wouldn't you rather a philosopher than a brick mason? Wouldn't you rather a poet than an undertaker? And wouldn't you rather make a donation than pay a fee? And why would it possibly make any difference?

And why only lethal injection or poison gas? Why not hanging? It's tidy enough. "Stand here. Chin up. There now. Press here." Or why not electrocution? "Sit here. Relax. Take a deep breath. Press here." Or those little but lethal hand-held air hammers they use in the slaughter house for cattle on kill day? "Look up, close your eyes, now squeeeeeeze." And why, for crissakes, why not guns? They've more than proven themselves reliable. They are the weapon of choice for most of the century. Why not pearl-handled, silver-bulleted, hair-triggered, .22 caliber Smith & Wessons? Pressed under the right earlobe, the entrance wound is tiny, the severence of the spinal cord is immediate and humane, and the exit wound, if indeed there is any, leaves no mess at all. Open caskets would be no problem. Perhaps a trash can lid, lined with bullet-proof netting could be held by the patient in his or her left hand to catch the debris and the silver bullet. It could be called, in the style of Dr. Kevorkian's wordsmithing, a *Sanitron*. Would there be any market for these bullets and shell casings, set tastefully in commemorative pendants or earrings or ankle bracelets, for surviving family members? Would people be willing to pay for such things?

And why only the terminally ill? If there is a right to die, a right to death with dignity, a right to be free of meaningless existence, free of pain and torment and tortuous hurt, then who gets to say that right belongs to some of the citizenry and not to all of it. Why not alcoholics? Why not the adult children of alcoholics? Why not the teenage grandchildren of alcoholics? Why not victims of sexual abuse or spousal abuse, of broken marriages or broken hearts or tax audits? Is their pain not real? Is their torment unworthy? Is there someone in the court or the congress or the church who has the say about which painful case is painful enough? Do we treat terminal people or terminal parts?

If the courts have broadly interpreted "the life of the mother" clause of their abortion rulings to include the economic life of the mother, the social life of the mother, the emotional life of the mother, the educational life of the mother, in order to extend the term and circumstances under which a woman might legally seek to terminate her pregnancy, should we reasonably expect the same courts to limit the exercise of a right to assisted suicide to anything narrower than life itself, which is, demonstrably, a terminal condition? And since my daughter is equally vulnerable to deadly depression as she is to unwanted pregnancy, is it wishful thinking to suppose she'd have to seek parental consent for the termination of one and not the other? Is she not entitled to privacy? Autonomy? Equal protection under the law?

And why all these women? Is there a message there? Before Dr. Jack, nine out of ten attempted suicides were women while five out of every six successful (maybe "completed" is a better word) suicides were men. Men were simply better at it. Unless, of course, one figures (on the axiom that a negative multiplied by a negative renders a positive) that failure at suicide is the mathematical equivalent of success. But among Kevorkian's devoted fatalities, fully seventy-five percent are women. Their average age of fifty-seven years situating them on one edge or the other of the empty nest and menopause. Is this the leveled playing field or gendercide? Is it sexism or affirmative action? Playing favorites or gender-norming? Or is it one of those Women's Issues men are supposed to keep quiet about, the way they were told to about abortion, as if it were the gender, not the species that reproduces.

Hard pressed to explain the imbalance himself, Dr. Jack, with characteristic indifference to his audience says, "It just seems that the ladies were asking for it." The truth perhaps, but told in the impolitic idioms of an age of chivalry and cardigan sweaters by a late-century, oddly cavalier, heroically challenged idealogue.

Are these the messes, the really bad ones, now: the questions we'd rather nobody asked?

The answers we each have are only our own. In the best case scenario, a majority rules. The majority can be dead wrong, of course, and often is. It's the chance one takes on democracy. But just as we can't only have the abortions we want or understand or could defend, we won't just have the "easy" assisted suicides. For every victim of rape or incest or life-threatening pregnancy who seeks an abortion there are several victimized by inconvenience or financial difficulties or emotional vexations. For every pain-wracked cancer patient there will be several deeply melancholic or acutely disturbed or bitterly indifferent but otherwise able-bodied applicants for assisted suicide. And just as we can't withhold the guaranteed abortion rights of a woman aborting one of twin fetuses because she doesn't feel she can afford two babies, emotionally or financially, we will not be able to withhold the guaranteed rights to assisted suicide to the young father who loses a job or the young woman who finds her husband in love with another. Where abortion is available on demand, should we really expect to moderate or regulate assisted suicide?

Where choice is enshrined we must suffer the choices.

Where life is sacred we must suffer the life.

Unvexed by the existentials, should we not expect the marketplace to take over? The questions devolve from *whether or not* to *who is entitled* to *who's going to pay* to *cash or charge?* to *do you take American Express?*

Of course, I can be wrong, too, and often am.

And I am preparing for the possibility. Both Dr. Jack and I are thinking of clinics—*obitoria* he calls them—because if I cannot beat him, I can surely compete with him. I can out-kevork him. It's good for everyone. It keeps the prices down. And my guess is that once he has made his point, he'll be too busy with talk shows and lecture tours to really stay home and take care of business.

I confess it has occured to me that a tastefully unimposing annex to my current emporium here in Milford might be the obvious and proximate preference of my townspeople. Two or three thousand barrier-free, nonthreatening square feet, say, with plenty of big pillows in earthtone natural fabrics, a kind of "parlor" with New Age music piped in, a staff of appropriately frumpy helping professionals trained to assist with "end of life" (the locally fashionable euphemism) decisions, exclusively motivational wall-treatments (*Love is Forever* or *Just Do It* imposed on a watercolor landscape of the Dolemites), reminiscent in decor and concordance of nothing so much as one's kindergarten classroom. And maybe a two- or three-unit crematorium attached, since, if we can believe the records here in Oakland County, nine out of every ten assisted suicides is burned. Of course, in our obitorium, we'd offer choices—about disposition of the body, caskets, urns, types of services, officiants, music. Along with traditional burnings and burials, we'd offer scatterings in outer space, or virtual entombments in cyberspace. And certainly the method of medicide should be a choice—pistols or poisons or plastic bags, hangings or bridge jumps or natural gas, and whether to do it on-site or at home or in one of our several designer locations—we have gardens, waterfalls, parks, and gazebos, all within walking distance. And whether to video or not is, naturally, a personal decision. And there would be several easy payment plans from which to, well, choose.

By a happy coincidence, our current holdings here in Milford take up most of a block at the corner of Liberty and First Streets, making *The First Liberty Clinic* an aptly patriotic, almost churchy corporate name. Or maybe just *The Libertorium*? Or how about *Serenity Social Services, Inc.*—Triple S, again. *Don't leave a mess, etcetera.*

Then someone will have to be in charge of establishing federally mandated minimum standards for Meaningful Living, below which, it might prudently follow, Social Security checks will be discontinued. Once life is meaningless, it oughtn't to be a burden on the taxpayers. And just as our generation of policymakers has found that abortion is more cost effective than paying welfare, our children's generation (already in arrears with our national debt) will find Medicide far better a bargain than Medicare. This will not *require* anyone to take their voluntary leave of this life, but it may help to *educate* them as to their options/duties as a citizen. I bet there'll be no shortage of bishops and politicos and actuarial agents in the next generation willing to serve on such a panel.

"The slippery-slope argument!" someone always says—as if to name it is to nullify it. As if things *don't* go from bad to worse. As if gravity did not exist.

Most of us just want to keep our balance.

Except, of course, for Dr. Kevorkian, whom history will record as a prophet. His attorney has suggested a Nobel Prize. His oils on canvas are all the rage. Can his own talk show be far behind?

Maybe Uncle Eddie was right all along. Maybe the handwriting's on the wall. Maybe it's only a matter of time. Maybe it's not worth bothering over. He seems happier. He gets more sleep. He has more time to spend with the family. He has no regrets.

He seems resigned to his decision to shut down Triple S. He gave away the novelty items, split the checkbook with his wife, his golfing buddy, and his golfing buddy's wife. He had the 800 number disconnected. And one night, months later, puzzling with the letters of its now familiar digits, he noticed how they might have spelled NOTHING. Nothing at all.

Jessica, the Hound and the Casket Trade

⌒

This would normally be the place to say (as critics of the American funeral trade invariably do), "I am not, of course, speaking of the vast majority of ethical funeral directors." But the vast majority of ethical funeral directors is precisely the subject of this book.

—JESSICA MITFORD, *THE AMERICAN WAY OF DEATH*, FOREWORD, P. VIII

She went to a long-established, "reputable" undertaker. Seeking to save the widow expense, she chose the cheapest redwood casket in the establishment and was quoted a low price. Later, the salesman called her back to say the brother-in-law was too tall to fit into this casket, she would have to take the one that cost $100 more. When my friend objected, the salesman said, "Oh, all right, we'll use the redwood one, but we'll have to cut off his feet."

—*IBID.* CHAPTER TWO, P. 24

The same mortician who once said he'd rather give away caskets than take advantage of someone in grief later hung billboards out by the interstate—a bosomy teenager in a white bikini over which it read *Better Bodies by Bixby* (not the real name) and the phone numbers for his several metro locations.

I offer this in support of the claim that there are good days and there are bad ones.

No less could be said for many of the greats.

I'm thinking of Hemingway's take on Pound when he said, "Ezra was right half the time, and when he was wrong, he was so wrong you were never in any doubt of it." But ought we be kept from "The River-Merchant's Wife" by his mistaken politics? Should outrage silence the sublime?

The same may be asked of Mr. Bixby's two memorable utterances.

Or, as a priest I've long admired once said, "Prophesy, like poetry, is a part-time job—the rest of the time they were only trying to keep their feet out their mouths." I suppose he was trying to tell me something.

Indeed, mine is an occupation that requires two feet firmly on the ground, less for balance, I often think, than to keep one or the other from angling toward its true home in my craw.

I sell caskets and embalm bodies and direct funerals.

Pollsters find among the general public a huge ambivalence about funeral directors. "I hope you'll understand it if I never want to see you again," the most satisfied among my customers will say. I understand.

And most of the citizenry, stopped on the street, would agree that funeral directors are mainly crooks, "except for mine . . . ," they just as predictably add. "The one who did my (*insert primary relation*) was really helpful, really cared, treated us like family."

This tendency, to abhor the general class while approving of the particular member is among the great human prerogatives—as true of clergy and senators as it is of teachers and physicians. Much the same could be said of Time: "Life sucks," we say, "but there was this moment . . . ," or of racial groups: "Some of my best friends are (*insert minority*) . . . ," or of gender: "(*Insert sex*)! You can't live with them and you can't live without them!"

Of course, there are certain members of the subspecies—I'm thinking lawyers, politicians, revenue agents—who are, in general and in particular, beyond redemption and we like it that way. "The devil you know's better than the one you don't . . . " is the best we can say about politicians. And who among us wants a "nice" divorce attorney or has even one fond memory involving the tax man? Really, now.

But back to caskets and bodies and funerals.

When it comes to caskets I'm very careful. I don't tell folks what they should or shouldn't do. It's bad form and worse for business. I tell them I don't have any that will get them into heaven or keep them out. There's none that turns a prince into a frog or, regrettably, vice-versa. There isn't a casket that compensates for neglect nor one that hides true love, honorable conduct, or affection.

If worth can be measured by what they do, it might help to figure out what caskets "do" in the inanimate object sense of the verb.

How many here are thinking "handles"? When someone dies, we try to get a handle on it. This is because dead folks don't move. I'm not making this part up. Next time someone in your house quits breathing, ask them to get up and answer the phone or maybe get you some ice water or let the cat out. He won't budge. It's because he's dead.

There was a time when it was easier to change caves than to drag the dead guy out. Now it's not so easy. There's the post office, the utilities, the closing costs. Now we have to remove the dead. The sooner the better is the rule of thumb, though it's not the thumb that will make this known.

This was a dour and awful chore, moving the dead from place to place. And like most chores, it was left to women to do. Later, it was discovered to be a high honor—to *bear the pall* as a liturgical role required a special place in the procession, special conduct, and often a really special outfit. When hauling the dead hither and yon became less a chore and more an honor, men took it over with enthusiasm.

In this it resembles the history of the universe. Much the same happened with protecting against the marauding hordes, the provision of meaty protein sources, and more recently, in certain highly specialized and intricate evolutions of food preparation and child care.

If you think women were at least participant and perhaps instrumental in the discovery of these honors, you might better keep such suspicions to yourself. These are not good days to think such thoughts.

But I stray again. Back to business.

Another thing you'll see most every casket doing is being horizontal. This is because the folks that make them have taken seriously the demonstrated preference of our species to do it on the level. Oh, sure—it can be done standing up or in a car or even upside down. But most everyone goes looking for something flat. Probably this can be attributed to gravity or physics or fatigue.

So horizontal things that can be carried—to these basic properties, we could add a third: it should be sturdy enough for a few hundred pounds. I'm glad that it's not from personal experience that I say that nothing takes the steam out of a good funeral so much as the bottom falling out.

And how many of you haven't heard of this happening?

A word on the words we're most familiar with.

Coffins are the narrow, octagonal fellows—mostly wooden, nicely corresponding to the shape of the human form before the advent of the junk food era. There are top and bottom, and the screws that fasten the one to the other are often ornamental. Some have handles, some do not, but all can be carried. The lids can be opened and closed at will.

Caskets are more rectangular and the lids are hinged and the body can be both carried and laid out in them. Other than shape, coffins and caskets are pretty much the same. They've been made of wood and metal and glass and ceramics and plastics and cement and the dear knows what else. Both are made in a range of prices.

But *casket* suggests something beyond basic utility, something about the contents of the box. The implication is that it contains something precious: heirlooms, jewels, old love letters, remnants and icons of something dear.

So casket is to coffin as tomb is to cave, grave is to hole in the ground, pyre is to bonfire. You get the drift? Or as, for example, eulogy is to speech, elegy to poem, home is to house, or husband to man. (I love this part, I get carried away.)

But the point is a *casket* presumes something about what goes in it. It presumes the dead body is important to someone. For some this will seem like stating the obvious. For others, I'm guessing, maybe not.

But when buildings are bombed or planes fall from the sky, or wars are won or lost, the bodies of the dead are really important. We want them back to let them go again—on our terms, at our pace, to say you may not leave without permission, forgiveness, our respects—to say we want our chance to say goodbye.

Both coffins and caskets are boxes for the dead. Both are utterly suitable to the task. Both cost more than most other boxes.

It's because of the bodies we put inside them. The bodies of mothers and fathers and sons, daughters and sisters and brothers and friends, the ones we knew and loved or knew and hated, or hardly knew at all, but know someone who knew them and who is left to grieve.

In 1906, John Hillenbrand, the son of a German immigrant bought the failing Batesville Coffin Company in the southeastern Indiana town of the same name. Following the form of the transportation industry, he moved from a primarily wooden product to products of metal that would seal against the elements. *Permanence* and *protection* were concepts that Batesville marketed successfully during and after a pair of World Wars in which men were being sent home in government boxes. The same wars taught different lessons to the British, for whom the sight of their burial grounds desecrated by bombs at intervals throughout the first half century suggested permanence and protection were courtesies they could no longer guarantee to the dead. Hence, the near total preference for cremation there.

Earth burial is practiced by "safe" societies and by settled ones. It presumes the dead will be left their little acre and that the living will be around to tend the graves. In such climates the fantasies of permanence and protection thrive. And the cremation rate in North America has risen in direct relation to the demographics and geographics of mobility and fear and the ever more efficient technologies of destruction.

The idea that a casket should be sealed against air and moisture is important to many families. To others it means nothing. They are both right. No one need to explain why it doesn't matter. No one need explain why it does. But Batesville, thinking that it might, engineered the first "sealed" casket with a gasket in the 1940s and made it available in metal caskets in every price range from the .20 gauge steels to the coppers and bronzes. One of the things they learned is that ninety-six percent of the human race would fit in a casket with interior dimensions of six feet six by two feet high by two feet wide—give or take.

Once they had the size figured out and what it was that people wanted in a casket—protection and permanence—then the rest was more or less the history of how the Hillenbrand brothers managed to make more and sell more than any of their competition. And they have. You see them in the movies, on the evening news being carried in and out of churches, at gravesides, being taken from hearses. If someone's in a casket in North America chances are better than even it's a Batesville.

We show twenty-some caskets to pick from. They're samples only. There are plenty more we can get within a matter of hours. What I carry in blue, my brother Tim, in the next town, carries in pink. What I carry tailored, Tim carries shirred. He carries one with the Last Supper on it. I've got one with the Pietà. One of his has roses on the handles. One of mine has sheaves of wheat.

You name it, we've got it. We aim to please.

We have a cardboard box (of a kind used for larger appliances) for seventy-nine dollars. We also have a mahogany box (of a kind used for Kennedys and Nixons and Onassises) for nearly eight grand. Both can be carried and buried and burned. Both will accommodate all but the tallest or widest citizens, for whom, alas, as in life, the selection narrows. And both are available to any customer who can pay the price.

Because a lot of us tend to avoid the extremes, regardless of how we elect to define them, we show a wide range of caskets in between and it would look on a chart like one of those bell curves: with the most in the middle and the least at either end. Thus, we show three oak caskets and only one mahogany, a bronze, a copper, a stainless steel, and six or seven regular steels of various gauges or thicknesses. We show a cherry, a maple, two poplars, an ash, a pine, a particle board, and the cardboard box. The linings are velvet or crepe or linen or satin, in all different colors, tufted or ruffled or tailored plain. You get pretty much what you pay for here.

I should probably fess up that we buy these caskets for less than we sell them for—a fact uncovered by one of our local TV news personalities, who called himself the News Hound, and who was, apparently, untutored in the economic intrigues of wholesale and retail. It was this same News Hound who did an expose on Girl Scout Cookie sales—how some of the money doesn't go to the girls at all, but to the national office where it was used to pay the salaries of "staff."

It was a well-worn trail the News Hound was sniffing—a trail blazed most profitably by Jessica Mitford who came to the best-selling if not exactly original conclusion that the bereaved consumer is in a bad bargaining position. When you've got a dead body on your hands it's hard to shop around. It's hard to shop lawyers when you're on the lam, or doctors when your appendix is inflamed. It's not the kind of thing you let out to bids.

Lately there has been a great push toward "pre-arrangement." Everyone who's anyone seems to approve. The funeral directors figure it's money in the bank. The insurance people love it since most of the funding is done through insurance. The late Jessica, the former News Hound, the anti-extravagance crowd—they all reckon it is all for the best to make such decisions when heads are cool and hearts are unencumbered by grief and guilt. There's this hopeful fantasy that by pre-arranging the funeral, one might be able to pre-feel the feelings, you know, get a jump on the anger and the fear and the helplessness. It's as modern as planned parenthood and pre-nuptial agreements and as useless, however tidy it may be about the finances, when it comes to the feelings involved.

And we are uniformly advised "not to be a burden to our children." This is the other oft-cited *bonne raison* for making your final arrangements in advance—to spare them the horror and pain of having to do business with someone like me.

But if we are not to be a burden to our children, then to whom? The government? The church? The taxpayers? Whom? Were they not a burden to us—our children? And didn't the management of that burden make us feel alive and loved and helpful and capable?

And if the planning of a funeral is so horribly burdensome, so fraught with possible abuses and gloom, why should an arthritic septuagenarian with blurred vision and some hearing loss be sent to the front to do battle with the undertaker instead of the forty-something heirs-apparent with their power suits and web browsers and cellular phones? Are they not far better outfitted to the task? Is it not their inheritance we're spending here? Are these not decisions they will be living with?

Maybe their parents do not trust them to do the job properly.

Maybe they shouldn't.

Maybe they should.

The day I came to Milford, Russ Reader started pre-arranging his funeral. I was getting my hair cut when I first met him. He was a massive man still, in his fifties, six-foot-something and four hundred pounds. He'd had, in his youth, a spectacular career playing college and professional football. His reputation had preceded him. He was a "character"—known in these parts for outrageous and libertine behavior. Like the Sunday he sold a Ford coupe off the used car lot uptown, taking a cash deposit of a thousand dollars and telling the poor customer to "come by in the morning when the office is open" for the keys and paperwork. That Russ was not employed by the car dealer—a devout Methodist who kept holy his Sabbaths—did not come to light before the money had been spent on sirloins and cigars and round after round of drinks for the patrons of Ye Olde Hotel—visiting matrons from the Eastern Star, in town with their husbands for a regional confab. Or the time a neighbor's yelping poodle—a dog disliked by everyone in earshot—was found shot one afternoon during Russ's nap time. The neighbor started screaming at one of Russ's boys over the back fence, "When I get my hands on your father!" Awakened by the fracas, Russ appeared at the upstairs window and calmly promised, "I'll be right down, Ben." He came down in his paisley dressing gown, decked the neighbor with a swift left hook, instructed his son to bury "that dead mutt," and went back upstairs to finish his nap. Halloween was Russ's favorite holiday, and he celebrated in more or less pre-Christian fashion, dressing himself up like a Celtic warrior, with an antlered helmet and mighty sword that, along with his ponderous bulk and black beard and booming voice, would scare the bejaysus out of the wee trick-or-treaters who nonetheless were drawn to his porch by stories of full-sized candy bars sometimes wrapped in five-dollar bills. Russ Reader was, in all ways, bigger than life, so that the hyperbole that attended the gossip about him was like the talk of heros in the ancient Hibernian epics—Cuchulainn and Deirdre and Queen Maeve, who were given to warp-spasms, wild couplings, and wondrous appetites.

When he first confronted me in the barber's chair, he all but blotted out the sun behind him.

"You're the new Digger O'Dell I take it."

It was the black suit, the wing rips, the gray striped tie.

"Well, you're never getting your mitts on my body!" he challenged.

The barber stepped back to busy himself among the talcums and clippers, uncertain of the direction the conversation might take.

I considered the size of the man before me—the ponderous bulk of him, the breathtaking mass of him—and tried to imagine him horizontal and uncooperative. A sympathetic pain ran down my back. I winced.

"What makes you think I'd want anything to do with your body?" I countered in a tone that emphasized my indignation.

Russ and I were always friends after that.

He told me he intended to have his body donated to "medical science." He wanted to be given to the anatomy department of his alma mater, so that fledgling doctors could practice on him.

"Won't cost my people a penny."

When I told him they probably wouldn't take him, on account of his size, he seemed utterly crestfallen. The supply of cadavers for medical and dental schools in this land of plenty was shamefully but abundantly provided for by the homeless and helpless, who were, for the most part, more "fit" than Russ was.

"But I was an all-American there!" Russ pleaded.

"Don't take my word for it," I advised. "Go ask for yourself."

Months later I was watering impatiens around the funeral home when Russ screeched to a halt on Liberty Street.

"OK, listen. Just cremate me and have the ashes scattered over town from one of those hot-air balloons." I could see he had given this careful thought. "How much will it cost me, bottom line?"

I told him the fees for our minimum services—livery and paperwork and a box.

"I don't want a casket," he hollered from the front seat of his Cadillac, idling at curbside now.

I explained we wouldn't be using a casket as such, still he would have to be *in* something. The crematory people wouldn't accept his body unless it was *in* something. They didn't *handle* dead bodies without some kind of handles. This made tolerable sense to Russ. In my mind I was thinking of a shipping case—a kind of covered pallet compatible with fork-lifts and freight handlers—that would be sufficient to the task.

"I can only guess at what the balloon ride will cost, Russ. It's likely to be the priciest part. And, of course, you'd have to figure on inflation. Are you planning to do this very soon?"

"Don't get cute with me, Digger," he shouted. "Whadayasay? Can I count on you?"

I told him it wasn't me he'd have to count on. He'd have to convince his wife and kids—the nine of them. They were the ones I'd be working for.

"But it's *my* funeral! *My* money."

Here is where I explained to Russ the subtle but important difference between the "adjectival" and "possessive" applications of the first-person singular pronoun for ownership—a difference measured by one's last breath. I explained that it was really *theirs* to do—his survivors, his family. It was really, listen closely, "the heirs"—the money, the funeral, what was or wasn't done with his body.

"I'll pay you now," he protested. "In cash—I'll pre-arrange it all. Put it in my Will. They'll have to do it the way I want it."

I encouraged Russ to ponder the worst-case scenario: his wife and his family take me to court. I come armed with his Last Will and pre-need documents insisting that his body get burned and tossed from a balloon hovering over the heart of town during Sidewalk Sale Days. His wife Mary, glistening with real tears, his seven beautiful daughters with hankies in hand, his two fine sons, bearing up manfully, petition the court for permission to lay him out, have the preacher in, bury him up on the hill where they can visit his grave whenever the spirit moves them to.

"Who do you think wins that one, Russ? Go home and make your case with them."

I don't know if he ever had that conversation with them all. Maybe he just gave up. Maybe it had all been for my consumption. I don't know. That was years ago.

When Russ died last year in his easy chair, a cigar smoldering in the ashtray, one of those evening game shows flickering on the TV, his son came to my house to summon me. His wife and his daughters were weeping around him. His children's children watched and listened. We brought the hearse and waited while each of the women kissed him and left. We brought the stretcher in and, with his sons' help, moved him from the chair, then out the door and to the funeral home where we embalmed him, gave him a clean shave, and laid him out, all of us amazed at how age and infirmity had reduced him so. He actually fit easily into a Batesville casket—I think it was cherry, I don't remember.

But I remember how his vast heroics continued to grow over two days of wake. The stories were told and told again. Folks wept and laughed outloud at his wild antics. And after the minister, a woman who'd known Russ all her life and had braved his stoop on Halloween, had had her say about God's mercy and the size of Heaven, she invited some of us to share our stories about Russ. After that we followed a brass band, holding forth with "When the Saints Go Marching In," to the grave. And after everything had been said that could be said, and done that could be done, Mary and her daughters went home to the embraces of neighbors and the casseroles and condolences, and Russ's sons remained to bury him. They took off their jackets, undid their ties, broke out a bottle and dark cigars and buried their father's body in the ground that none of us thought it would ever fit into. I gave the permit to the sexton and left them to it.

And though I know his body is buried there, something of Russ remains among us now. Whenever I see hot-air balloons—fat flaming birds adrift in the evening air—I sense his legendary excesses raining down on us, old friends and family—his blessed and elect—who duck our heads or raise our faces to the sky and laugh or catch our breath or cry.

In even the best of caskets, it never all fits—all that we'd like to bury in them: the hurt and forgiveness, the anger and pain, the praise and thanksgiving, the emptiness and exaltations, the untidy feelings when someone dies. So I conduct this business very carefully because, in the years since I've been here, when someone dies, they never call Jessica or the News Hound.

They call me.

Tract

❧

Share with us—it will be money
in your pockets.
Go now
I think you are ready.

—WILLIAM CARLOS WILLIAMS, "TRACT"

I'd rather it be February. Not that it will matter much to me. Not that I'm a stickler for details. But since you're asking— February. The month I first became a father, the month my father died. Yes. Better even than November.

I want it cold. I want the gray to inhabit the air like wood does trees: as an essence not a coincidence. And the hope for springtime, gardens, romance, dulled to a stump by the winter in Michigan.

Yes, February. With the cold behind and the cold before you and the darkness stubborn at the edges of the day. And a wind to make the cold more bitter. So that ever after it might be said, "It was a sad old day we did it after all."

And a good frosthold on the ground so that, for nights before it is dug, the sexton will have had to go up and put a fire down, under the hood that fits the space, to soften the topsoil for the backhoe's toothy bucket.

Wake me. Let those who want to come and look. They have their reasons. You'll have yours. And if someone says, "Doesn't he look natural!" take no offense. They've got it right. For this was always in my nature. It's in yours.

And have the clergy take their part in it. Let them take their best shot. If they're ever going to make sense to you, now's the time. They're looking, same as the rest of us. The questions are more instructive than the answers. Be wary of anyone who knows what to say.

As for music, suit yourselves. I'll be out of earshot, stone deaf. A lot can be said for pipers and tinwhistlers. But consider the difference between a funeral with a few tunes and a concert with a corpse down front. Avoid, for your own sakes, anything you've heard in the dentist's office or the roller rink.

Poems might be said. I've had friends who were poets. Mind you, they tend to go on a bit. Especially around horizontal bodies. Sex and death are their principal studies. It is here where the services of an experienced undertaker are most appreciated. Accustomed to being *personae non grata*, they'll act the worthy editor and tell the bards when it's time to put a sock in it.

On the subject of money: you get what you pay for. Deal with someone whose instincts you trust. If anyone tells you you haven't spent enough, tell them to go piss up a rope. Tell the same thing to anyone who says you spent too much. Tell them to go piss up a rope. It's your money. Do what you want with it. But let me make one thing perfectly clear. You know the type who's always saying "When I'm dead, save your money, spend it on something really useful, do me cheaply"? I'm not one of them. Never was. I've always thought that funerals were useful. So do what suits you. It is yours to do. You're entitled to wholesale on most of it.

As for guilt—it's much overrated. Here are the facts in the case at hand: I've known the love of the ones who have loved me. And I've known that they've known that I've loved them, too. Everything else, in the end, seems irrelevant. But if guilt is the thing, forgive yourself, forgive me. And if a little upgrade in the pomp and circumstance makes you feel better, consider it money wisely spent. Compared to shrinks and pharmaceuticals, bartenders or homeopaths, geographical or ecclesiastical cures, even the priciest funeral is a bargain.

I want a mess made in the snow so that the earth looks wounded, forced open, an unwilling participant. Forego the tent. Stand openly to the weather. Get the larger equipment out of sight. It's a distraction. But have the sexton, all dirt and indifference, remain at hand. He and the hearse driver can talk of poker or trade jokes in whispers and straight-face while the clergy tender final commendations. Those who lean on shovels and fill holes, like those who lean on custom and old prayers, are, each of them, experts in the one field.

And you should see it till the very end. Avoid the temptation of tidy leavetaking in a room, a cemetery chapel, at the foot of the altar. None of that. Don't dodge it because of the weather. We've fished and watched football in worse conditions. It won't take long. Go to the hole in the ground. Stand over it. Look into it. Wonder. And be cold. But stay until it's over. Until it is done.

On the subject of pallbearers—my darling sons, my fierce daughter, my grandsons and granddaughters, if I've any. The larger muscles should be involved. The ones we use for the real burdens. If men and their muscles are better at lifting, women and theirs are better at bearing. This is a job for which both may be needed. So work together. It will lighten the load.

Look to my beloved for the best example. She has a mighty heart, a rich internal life, and powerful medicines.

After the words are finished, lower it. Leave the ropes. Toss the gray gloves in on top. Push the dirt in and be done. Watch each other's ankles, stamp your feet in the cold, let your heads sink between your shoulders, keep looking down. That's where what is happening is happening. And when you're done, look up and leave. But not until you're done.

So, if you opt for burning, stand and watch. If you cannot watch it, perhaps you should reconsider. Stand in earshot of the sizzle and the pop. Try to get a whiff of the goings on. Warm your hands to the fire. This might be a good time for a song. Bury the ashes, cinders, and bones. The bits of the box that did not burn.

Put them in something.

Mark the spot.

Feed the hungry. It's good form. Feed them well. This business works up an appetite, like going to the seaside, walking the cliff road. After that, be sober.

This is none of my business. I won't be there. But if you're asking, here is free advice. You know the part where everybody is always saying that you should have a party now? How the dead guy always insisted he wanted everyone to have a good time and toss a few back and laugh and be happy? I'm not one of them. I think the old teacher is right about this one. There *is* a time to dance. And it just may be this isn't one of them. The dead can't tell the living what to feel.

They used to have this year of mourning. Folks wore armbands, black clothes, played no music in the house. Black wreathes were hung at the front doors. The damaged were identified. For a full year you were allowed your grief—the dreams and sleeplessness, the sadness, the rage. The weeping and giggling in all the wrong places. The catch in your breath at the sound of the name. After a year, you would be back to normal. "Time heals" is what was said to explain this. If not, of course, you were pronounced some version of "crazy" and in need of some professional help.

Whatever's there to feel, feel it—the riddance, the relief, the fright and freedom, the fear of forgetting, the dull ache of your own mortality. Go home in pairs. Warm to the flesh that warms you still. Get with someone you can trust with tears, with anger, and wonderment and utter silence. Get that part done—the sooner the better. The only way around these things is through them.

I know I shouldn't be going on like this.

I've had this problem all my life. Directing funerals.

It's yours to do—my funeral—not mine. The death is yours to live with once I'm dead.

So here is a coupon good for Disregard. And here is another marked My Approval. Ignore, with my blessings, whatever I've said beyond Love One Another.

Live Forever.

All I really wanted was a witness. To say I was. To say, daft as it still sounds, maybe I *am*.

To say, if they ask you, it was a sad day after all. It was a cold, gray day.

February.

Of course, any other month you're on your own. Have no fear—you'll know what to do. Go now, I think you are ready.

Notes on Frontispieces

Page 1:   Black and white photograph of Moyarta Cemetery near Carrigaholt, County Clare.

Page 15:   Black and white photograph of Rosemary and Edward Lynch on the beach in St. Thomas, U.S. Virgin Islands, 1963.

Page 27:   Detail of street map, Galway City.

Page 43:   "St. Stephen." Illustration from *Lives of the Saints for Every Day of the Year*, Rev. Hugo Hoever, S.O.Cist., Ph.D., editor, 1955. Catholic Book Publishing Co., New York.

Page 59:   "Artichoke." Black and white photograph by Patrick Young.

Page 75:   Black and white photo of page from Kelco Supply Catalogue featuring a cultured walnut golf bag cremation urn with smaller "keepsake" golf bag on its own fairway. Courtesy of Kelco Supply Company.

Page 101:   Black and white photograph of Oak Grove Cemetery, Milford, Michigan. Photo courtesy of Patrick Young.

Page 123:   Black and white photograph of pedestrian directional sign to "Hospitals" outside of Number 11 Dombey Street, London. Photo courtesy of Nico Sweeney.

Page 137: "Recumbent Woman." Charcoal and tempera on paper, 1996. Sean Lynch.

Page 149: Black and white photograph of left hand of suicide machine user from files of Oakland County Medical Examiner's office.

Page 177: "Details from the Casket Trade." Black and white photograph by M. E. Lynch.

Page 193: Black and white photograph of curbside stone from Lynch Vault in Moyarta Cemetery, Carrigaholt, County Clare.